EVERYTHING

WHLE$ALING

EVERYTHING

WH LE ALING

The Ultimate Guide to Wholesaling
Real Estate

By: Carol Stinson

Contents

Introduction

EVERYTHING WHOLESALING is a powerful guide to real estate profit that is packed with all of the information that you will ever need to make money in real estate with NO money, NO credit and NO risk!

Whether you're new to real estate wholesaling or an active wholesaler looking to take your wholesaling business to the highest level possible this book is for you.

This POWERFUL wholesaling guide contains all of the strategies that you will ever need to profit and be successful in today's real estate market. From traditional wholesaling strategies to new wholesaling strategies that are proven to be effective in today's real estate market, it's all in here.

Need help finding buyers, negotiating a deal or successfully close REOs and Short Sales… IT'S IN HERE! Need contracts? They're in here!

EVERYTHING WHOLESALING not only contains ALL of the basic wholesaling strategies, but also contains my strategies to successfully close REOs, Short sales and Foreclosures without the expense of a double close. I have even included how to successfully wholesale properties subject to the existing financing.

You will learn how to find estate properties before anyone else finds them, the strategies that I used to recruit over 7,000 buyers in 12 states and other powerful strategies that will increase your profit and keep you ahead of all of the other wholesalers and buyers in your area.

If your reading this that means that everything you will ever need to make money in real estate is in your hands. EVERYTHING WHOLESALING contains everything you need to find buyers, find properties, market your properties, negotiate and evaluate properties, build your power team, leverage the power of Land Trusts to close REOs and Short Sales and so much more.

Not only have I included all of my most effective wholesaling strategies but I went a step further to ensure your success. I am going to share MY WHOLESALING VAULT with you.

In the VAULT you will find...

1. Every contract that you will ever need to make every deal successful.
2. Videos for each contract explaining step by step how to fill out each section of the contract.
3. Step by step videos on how to leverage zillow, craigslist and more.
4. Hard Money & Transactional Funding Resources

5. NEW videos each month with new strategies and updated information on new wholesaling techniques as they develop with each market shift.

The EVERYTHING WHOLESALING GUIDE combined with MY WHOLESALING VAULT equals profit in any market at any time!

- **No more searching for wholesale strategies to get a deal closed.**

EVERY wholesaling strategy that you will EVER need will be at your fingertips!

- **No more struggling with how to fill out a particular contract.**

EVERY contract that you will EVER need to successfully transfer any real estate property over to your buyer will be in your WHOLESALING VAULT.

EVERY contract will even have a video on how to properly fill out each section of the contract!

- **No more deals left behind, EVER!**

EVERY creative wholesaling strategy that you will EVER need to ensure that EVERY deal gets closed will be in your wholesaling guide ready for you to utilize. Not only will you learn the step by step process to put each strategy into place, but you will have direct access to my WHOLESALING VAULT where you will find all of the contracts to make it happen and a video on how to fill out each contract!

I have closed over 650 wholesale deals using every creative wholesaling strategy known, even created a few myself, and I share them all with you in this book.

My wholesaling strategies work, they are effective in producing profit and now I want to share them with you so that you can take real estate wholesaling to a whole new level. With the strategies, resources and contracts contained in this book along with access to MY WHOLESALING VAULT you too can generate profit from real estate every single month.

There has never been a better time to profit from real estate than right now. Whether you're new to wholesaling or an experienced wholesaler EVERYTHING WHOLESALING is the only tool that you will ever need to profit in today's real estate market.

If you're serious about making money in real estate and are looking for powerful, effective strategies that are proven to work in today's crazy real estate market then EVERYTHING WHOLESALING has exactly what you need to make that happen.

Chapter 1

WHOLESALING BASICS

Wholesaling is a very effective strategy to make money in real estate with NO money and NO credit. Even if you have no prior knowledge of real estate you can quickly learn how to wholesale real estate and make a profit.

Real estate wholesaling will not make you wealthy, but it can make you rich as it is a great CASH NOW strategy. While real estate investing, purchasing properties, keeping them and renting them out, is a **wealth building strategy** as it provides an ongoing profit through the rent and equity of the property, wholesaling is a **fast cash strategy, a "make money now" strategy.**

When you make a profit, cash now, from wholesaling a property you must find and wholesale another property to make a profit again. But, if you buy and hold a property, rent it out, you will continuously earn money each month. This monthly income is called "cash flow" and over time can build wealth. Real estate investing is a wealth building strategy and real estate wholesaling is a "cash now" strategy.

However, real estate wholesaling can also produce a monthly income if you have a pipeline of properties, many properties under contract at one time, and a list of cash buyers you can make "CASH NOW" consistently every month.

The difference between a Real Estate Wholesaler and a Real Estate Agent.

One thing to keep in mind is that while Real Estate Agents sell properties Real Estate wholesalers do NOT sell properties, they sell contracts. Real estate wholesalers sell the purchase contract that they negotiate with the seller on a property not the property itself.

A wholesaler negotiates a property for sale with a seller, signs a purchase agreement contract with that seller and then sells the rights to that purchase agreement to a buyer. The buyer then pays the wholesaler a fee and takes over the purchase agreement contract between the seller and the wholesaler. The buyer will now step into the wholesalers place and buy the property.

There is much confusion about the position of the wholesaler. Many people feel that a wholesaler is a person selling houses without a license. Others feel that wholesaling is not legal or that wholesalers advertising a property for sale is illegal. This is a misconception that needs to be clarified.

Since the recent market drop there have been many new wholesalers jumping on the bandwagon to quick cash. This has allot of people questioning the position of the wholesaler and many Real Estate Agents are putting their guard up.

Real Estate Agents have a license to sell real estate because legally you need a license to sell real estate. Wholesalers do not need a license because they are not selling real estate they are selling their contract rights to a certain real estate property. Because contract rights are considered property, they can be transferred to others just like a piece of property such as a home or car.

A real estate wholesaler finds a property, negotiates the price with the seller and then has the seller sign an "Agreement to Purchase" contract. Since many wholesalers are also Real Estate Investors they will either choose to go through with the purchase and take title to the property or they will sell their rights to the property to another investor for a profit. This process is known as selling your equitable interest in a property or wholesaling real estate.

Once you have a property under contract with a seller, all rights of the contract is considered "property" and therefore under your control. Therefore you reserve the right to do what you want with it. The wholesaler who has a property listed for sale is not selling the property but their rights to buy the property that they have under contract with the owner of the property. Once you have the right to buy a property through a signed purchase agreement you have the right to sell your equitable interest in that property. Just to be sure you get it... **Wholesalers do not need a license because they are not selling real estate, they are selling their contractual right to a property.**

One other distinction between a realtor and a wholesaler is that the Realtor waits for the seller to come to them to list their properties and relies on the MLS (Multiple Listing Service) to sell their properties to buyers. The wholesaler, on the other hand, not only makes every effort to go out and find properties, but continuously recruits buyers for their wholesale deals by building their buyers list. A wholesaler focuses on developing two things: finding deals and their network of investors to sell their deals to.

In essence it truly does not matter what your position is in the real estate world. With the real estate market at an all-time low and foreclosures on the rise there has never been a better time to make money in real estate. Whether wholesaler or realtor you are sure to profit in today's market if you are determined to do so.

Is real estate wholesaling legal?

There are some who may tell you that real estate wholesaling is illegal and try to discourage you from doing it. The truth is that real estate wholesaling is a perfectly legal real estate investment strategy. Because contract rights are considered property, they can be transferred to others just like a piece of property such as a home or car.

Let's say you have a contract to purchase a number of items each month from a dealer, at a certain price. The contract runs for a year. You then decided the product is no longer working out for you, and you'd rather not buy any more. As long as your contract allows it, you can just find someone else who wants to buy the same number of items each month and sell your rights and obligations under the contract to him. You can do this by assigning your Purchase Agreement over to someone else who would like to buy the product.

Most contracts permit an assignment as long as the other party to the contract approves the assignment. And many contracts require the other party to approve of an assignment as long as the assignment is "reasonable," meaning that the assignment won't jeopardize the security of the other party or increase the other party's risks.

So in conclusion, what I have shared with you is that once you have a property under contract, all rights of the contract is considered "property" and therefore under your control. Therefore you reserve the right to do what you want with it. Assigning your right to purchase the property once it is under contract is your right. (lawyers.com)

"When we have the right to buy, we have the right to sell" Attorney William Bronchick – Real Estate Lawyer and Investor.

Building your team

Effective wholesaling is not a one man job. It's a team effort! As any effective wholesaler will tell you, you need to have a good team in place to help you get each deal to the closing table and make you money.

An effective wholesaling team consists of:

1. **A Real Estate Agent**

   A good, Investor friendly Agent, is a huge asset to the wholesaler. An Agent provides you with properties that are listed on the MLS, makes offers for you and because they are generally well connected to other real estate entities they are a great resource to have on your team.

2. **A closing entity**

   Whether your state uses a Title Co. or an Attorney when

closing real estate transactions you will need a closing entity that is familiar with wholesaling. Visit http://www.escrowhelp.com/state-by-state-closing-guide.html to see whether your state uses a Title Company or a closing Attorney to conduct real estate closings

3. **Property Locators** (Bird Dogs)

   The more people searching for properties for you the better. Property Locators are essential as they keep the property leads coming in.

Property Locators can be a huge asset to a Wholesaler. I post the following ad on craigslist to recruit my property locators.

Would you like to earn extra $$$ each month?

Local real estate Investors are looking for individuals to locate vacant and distressed properties. You could earn up to $4,000.00 per month locating these properties. FREE Training! Contact xxx-xxx-xxxx for more information.

A Property Locator ONLY gets paid if they bring you a property and you close on it.

4. **A Contractor**

   Having a good contractor on your team that is willing to help you with rehab estimates is a bonus!

5. **A Property Management Co.**

   A local Property Management Co. is a great resource to

have when you are wholesaling rental properties.

Having the right team in place to take each deal from start to finish will help you keep a pipeline of good deals going. The more deals you have under contract the more money you will make!

NO money, NO credit and NO risk

The reasons why real estate wholesaling is a great strategy to use when starting out in real estate is because…

1. Real estate wholesaling does not require any of your own money to get started.

    - As you will learn, when you put a property under contract to buy you actually become the middle man. Therefore all of the funds needed to buy the property will come directly from a buyer that will ultimately step into your position in the transaction.

2. Real estate wholesaling never requires you to have a personal credit inquiry.

    - Since you are never actually purchasing the property you do not need to get a loan or a mortgage. Therefore your personal credit is never checked in any of the transactions.

3. Real estate wholesaling is risk free.

- All of the contracts that you will use in wholesaling contain "exit clauses" that allow you to get out of the contract should you have no success finding a buyer to step into your position. You will learn more about contracts and exit clauses in the following chapters.

This is why real estate wholesaling is the most effective strategy to make money in real estate. You can literally start wholesaling real estate flat broke with the worst credit in the world and start making a profit. There are no employment qualifications and the only job requirement is a willingness to learn, a desire to succeed and some motivation.

Understanding the motives of people

Real estate wholesaling is as much about people as it is about real estate. Aside from knowing the wholesaling process, success in wholesaling depends upon understanding the motives of people. What makes investors buy? What makes sellers sell? What makes sellers motivated enough to sell at a discount?

Most of the motives that you will encounter in real estate are based on at least four primal instincts:

1. To increase personal comforts and freedoms.
2. To be liked, respected, and esteemed by friends, family, and society.
3. To feel as if life has some meaning or purpose.
4. To nurture and protect family members even when they have passed away. As you will see when negotiating estate properties with the family.

These four primal instincts have an impact on real estate decisions made by sellers, buyers and even yourself. Your knowledge of these motives and being able to recognize them when they are present in your negotiations will enable you to know which deals are worth pursuing and which ones you need to walk away from.

For example there will be times when you may notice that a family member is still protecting their loved one on an estate property and unwilling to negotiate on the price. They may feel that their family member loved the home and therefore your offer disrespects their memory. That is a good indication that you need to walk away and give them some more time. Touch base with them again in 30 days and see how they are doing. You will be surprised how much things change once the bills start coming in and sometimes just giving them some extra time to grieve and accept their loss is enough.

Maybe your negotiating with a seller whose motive is to increase personal comforts and freedoms. If the seller is driven by this motive then it will be hard to get them down on their asking price as they have already spent that money in their head and they have BIG plans. They are seeking comfort and they are focused on nothing else. I generally walk away from a seller with this motive as it is impossible to negotiate with them to a price where you need them to be to create a deal.

As you begin to recognize the motives that drive seller and buyer decisions you will begin to see which properties are even worth your time pursuing. Your time is your most valuable asset, don't waste it chasing properties that will never become deals that make you money.

In the following chapters I will cover a few of these motives in more detail.

Points to remember:

1. You are not selling real estate so you do not need a license.
2. Real estate wholesaling is %100 legal.
3. Real estate wholesaling is a "cash now" strategy but can produce a monthly income with a pipeline of properties.
4. Real estate wholesaling is a team effort. With the right team you can be very successful.

Chapter 2

KNOW YOUR REAL ESTATE MARKET

Why would someone want to buy a house in your market? Are there new production plants opening up creating jobs? How about a new shopping center or a casino? Are there employment opportunities coming to your area? These are all questions that a buyer is going to consider before purchasing an investment property in your area.

Those who consistently make money in real estate know their real estate market. They know what new developments are planned, what the employment statistics are and the main roads that are used to commute to the closest city. They know the transportation and the schools. They know everything about the area where they invest. They have to know it all in order to make smart decisions regarding their real estate investments.

An experienced Investor is going to analyze an area to see if he will be able to sell his investment property to a home owner after he buys it and rehabs it. The Investor will take into consideration the schools, social classes and area development before he decides what area to purchase in. Because you will be looking to wholesale properties to Investors in these areas you should take the time to study your market and gain insight into the area.

One indication that a particular area is up-and-coming and worth the investment is the development of new roads and schools being built. This is a sign that the community is about to grow. Investing in a growing community can be very profitable.

You can do a quick research of any market using Google. Simply put the zip code and state of the market that you're interested in into the google search bar and Google will pull up all of the information that you need about a particular area. From current events to area development Google will let you know what is happening in a particular location.

You can also visit the municipality and speak with the zoning departments. They should be aware of any major projects that will be started in the area.

The most important thing that an Investor will research is the current price trends for the properties in the area. You should look to see if home prices are increasing in one area more than others. This will provide an idea of where the largest home buyer demand is.

You can research the real estate market trends in a particular area using various real estate websites. Zillow.com has allot to say about market trends and a particular real estate market. Actually this often underestimated web tool can quickly become the hub of your real estate investing career.

Zillow will give you a total run down of your investing area.

- Properties for sale
- Properties for rent
- Properties in foreclosure
- Price and tax history

Zillow will give you a visual market analysis of any real estate investing area in the country. If you are looking to buy a property on the West Coast and you're on the East Cost you can quickly search Zillow and see what's going on in the real estate market in ANY state.

If I get a deal on a particular street and I want to see what is for sale on that street, what is in foreclosure and what has sold recently

I automatically go to Zillow. This will give me a general idea of how fast my deal will sell at a particular price point. Granted I cannot predict if my deal will sell or not, but by researching the area I can get a pretty good feel of whether or not the deal that I am working with is worth my time.

Trulia.com is another great tool for market research. If you go to http://www.trulia.com/real_estate and put your zip code into the search bar it will bring up a market analysis of that market. This analysis will give you everything that you need from average home prices, most popular zip codes, school ratings and much more. Trulia is the most extensive and complete market analysis tool on the web. I strongly recommend that you utilize it when researching a particular market.

Employment and development

Take the time to research your market and see what is coming in the future. Find out if your County is planning any neighborhood development. Are they building a new park or putting in new pavements or street lights in a certain area? County renovations are always good signs that a certain area is about to be developed or improved. You can call your County Zoning office and ask them for any information on neighborhood development that will take place in the near future. You can also use the internet and Google to see if any job opportunities or neighborhood development is coming to your area.

Employment controls a market. It is the foundation of buying and selling in an area. If jobs get scarce people move out to find work. If jobs are coming to your area you can bet that people will start buying houses and moving in. People will buy where the jobs are and Investors buy where the people are buying.

Development is another thing that drives people to buy in a particular market. New housing, new shopping centers and even a new casino can bring people in. A new casino not only creates jobs, but the government requires that a certain amount of proceeds from a casino get put back into the community. This results in neighborhood improvements and development which results in higher housing prices and better investment opportunity.

It is very important that you take the time to study your market and learn as much as you can about the neighborhoods and housing market. Your knowledge of your market will be a great attribute to Investors looking to buy. You will be able to tell them where the hot markets are and why they should buy a property from you in a certain area.

It pays to do your homework and to determine which areas are hot now and, more importantly, which ones will be hot in the future. These are the areas where you need to be looking for properties, these are the areas where your buyers are buying. I guarantee that your buyers have already done their homework on the local market and have tunnel vision on a certain area. If you can find them property deals in these areas you will do well as a wholesaler.

Points to remember:

1. Research your real estate market.
    - Be aware of any community development.
    - Know the real estate market.
    - Know the economic and social conditions.
    - Know the school ratings

Chapter 3

FINDING PROPERTIES

As a Wholesaler finding properties must be your #1 priority. Searching for properties must be at the top of your "to do" list every day. Not just any properties, but properties that have the potential of becoming wholesale deals that make you money. These properties must all have one key ingredient "a motivated seller". This means that you must not only search for properties, but you must search for properties with a motivated seller for it to become a wholesale deal that will make you money.

How to recognize a motivated seller

I cannot begin to tell you how much time I have wasted trying to negotiate a deal with a seller who was simply not motivated to sell. I have met with hundreds of sellers, walked through countless properties only to find out in the end that the seller was not motivated enough to negotiate on the price. I would try to create motivation by showing the cost of repairs and explaining the property values of the surrounding properties only to realize that motivation cannot be created it had to be initiated. The seller must come into the deal with motivation for a deal to be profitable. You can NOT create a motivated seller!

I quickly realized that seller motivation is key to any real estate investment deal. If the seller of a property is not motivated there will never be a profitable real estate investment! With no motivation to sell the property the seller is willing to sit and wait until they get the price that they are asking for the property. If there is no desperation to sell, no urgent circumstances, the seller will never open up to your reasoning to discount the property enough to wholesale it and make profit.

I have learned to simply walk away if a deal lacks seller motivation. It's not worth my time and effort to negotiate a property if the seller is not motivated to sell. Therefore, I now determine the motivation level of a seller before I waste my time even looking at the property. I want to know their current reasoning for selling and the circumstances that led up to their decision to sell.

Let's face it, we all want to find those motivated sellers. Those property owners who simply need to make a deal with an **Investor** in order to unload their burden of a problem property. Therefore the first thing we must do as wholesalers or real estate investors is to understand what makes a **seller** motivated. What makes a seller so motivated that they are willing to negotiate the price in an effort to unload their burden property?

Below are some of the circumstances that can make a seller motivated enough to negotiate the purchase price and create a killer deal for you.

1. They desperately need to sell their property because of financial circumstances. The loss of a job, the death of a loved one etc… Something happened that changed their financial situation.

2. They are in an Adjustable Rate Mortgage and can no longer afford the increasing payments due to lack of employment or insufficient income.

3. They are in pre-foreclosure and need to sell their property to avoid an inevitable foreclosure.

4. They must relocate to another state due to job transfer or military deployment.

5. The repairs needed on the property are more than they can afford.

Your success as a real estate investor or wholesaler depends on your ability to distinguish between a motivated seller and a non-motivated seller. You will never convince a non-motivated seller to turn into a motivated seller. You will be wasting valuable time trying to transform a seller who does not have current circumstances to make them motivated enough to make a deal.

The evidence of a motivated seller depends on the answer to three basic questions.

1. Would you sell your house for what you owe on it?

2. Would you let me buy your house by taking over the payments?

3. Would you be willing to owner finance the property with a small down payment?

If the seller answers "yes" to these questions they are truly motivated and you should be able to lock in a great deal. If they say "yes" to question 2 then you could possibly take over the property and continue making the mortgage payments with literally no money down. This process is known as buying a property *"subject to the existing financing"*. You will learn more about this strategy in the following chapters.

If a seller answers "no" to these questions then they are evidently not motivated and you will be wasting valuable time trying to negotiate. I suggest that you check back with this seller in 30 days as motivation can change over time. Continue to move on until you find that motivated seller that is willing to negotiate a great investment deal.

There are Real Estate Investment deals and then there are GREAT Real Estate Investment deals. A motivated seller is the difference between the two!

Now that you know how to identify a motivated seller we can start looking for properties.

20 Ways to find investment properties

1. Bandit Signs – hand written signs seem to get the best response. Post them at intersections or on phone poles in your area.

2. Classified Ads – Post "We Buy Houses" ads on craigslist and your local newspaper.

3. Vehicle Magnet Signs – Magnetic signs will advertise your message while you're driving.

4. Business Cards – Give your card to everyone! The mailman, the pizza delivery guy and anyone else who drives neighborhoods for a living. Tell them that you give a referral fee if they give you a lead on a vacant property and you are able to purchase it.

5. Door Hangers - Hang these on doors in your neighborhood. Make sure the message on the door hanger has your contact info and states that you buy houses.

6. Wear your message - "We Buy Houses" shirts, jackets, hats etc.

7. Driving for Dollars - Drive neighborhoods for vacant, condemned and boarded up houses.

8. Flyers - Post flyers in supermarket, laundry mat and in any other public place that allows it.

9. Website Marketing - Create a website that collects information from motivated sellers and provides information about your company.

10. Bird Dogs - Recruit others to send your property leads by offering to pay them a fee if you close on a property.

11. Billboards - Rent a local billboard in your area that will get your message across.

12. Town meetings- A great way to let the locals know what you are doing.

13. Direct Mail - Crafting a letter and or postcard and mailing them to targeted lists – Probates, Pre-Foreclosures etc.

14. Networking With Professionals - It's important to build your real estate network with professionals – people who work with real estate or work with people with real estate. Accountants, Lawyers, Appraisers, Realtors etc.

15. Insurance Companies - Fire damaged and un-insurable properties can be a source of profitable deals.

16. Property Management Companies - These companies could know ahead of time if a landlord is selling a property, if there are problem tenants and a problem property.

17. Department Of Code Enforcement -These are the people who will usually contact you for posting bandit signs but they also know which properties in town are condemned.

18. Estate, Moving And Garage Sales - Drive your area looking for yard sales and garage sales. These are sometimes homeowners preparing to move. Also check your local newspaper for Estate Sales, Garage Sales etc…

19. MLS - Have your Realtor Look for listings with keywords such as handyman special, motivated seller and properties that have been on the market for a long time.

20. Word Of Mouth Advertising - Let people know that you are looking for properties. Tell others what you do.

Driving for dollars

There are thousands of properties for sale at your fingertips. The newspaper, Online classifieds, and for sale by owner web sites. But those deals are at the fingertips of everyone else too. In today's struggling economy there are more wholesalers and bird dogs surfing the internet in search of deals than there have ever been before. I know wholesalers that search at work, on their lunch break and just about every free moment that they have for that perfect deal.

With so many wholesalers searching online this means that the best deals are those that are sitting right in your back yard. The deals that the other wholesalers will not find online. Many wholesalers have day jobs and are not able to bird dog the streets in search of a deal. This is why they search endlessly on the internet for their deals. You better believe that every deal posted on craigslist is getting emails or phone calls by wholesalers. I say do what the others are not doing! Find the deals waiting to be discovered right in your neighborhood.

I know your saying, *"wait a minute I have a day job too"*. I am not suggesting that you spend your whole day driving around. Simply leaving 30 minutes earlier for work or taking another route home to drive down side streets is enough to find a great deal. Make sure you keep your camera in the car so you can readily take pictures when you find a vacant property. Write down the address and research the owner when you get home. You will learn how to do this later in this chapter.

In today's market there are thousands of foreclosures sitting vacant across the Country. You can always identify a foreclosure or bank owned property by the paper taped to the front window or door. This paper identifies the bank that owns the property and the maintenance company that maintains the property. I always call the maintenance company first because they will have a specific name of a person that hired them from the bank to maintain the property. I will ask the maintenance company for that contact name and number so I can call them and inquire about the property.

When I call the bank contact I ask them if they are interested in selling the property for a "cash" price. Often times they will tell me that it is not listed for sale yet etc... I stay persistent and ask to speak to someone who can make the decision to sell the property even though it's not listed yet for sale. The banks are not in the business of holding properties they are in the business of lending money. So every property that sits vacant on their books lowers the amount of funds that they can lend to new mortgagees etc... They want to sell, you just have to convince the right person at the bank to sell to you.

If there is no foreclosure paper on the window then you must do a bit of research to find the owner. You will need to contact the owner and find out if the property is for sale.

To find the owner simply go to google.com and type in "(your state) tax records". Example "New Jersey tax records". If there is an online website it will save you from going down to the tax office every time you find a vacant property. Tax records are public record and will identify the owner of a property once you type in the property address.

Once you find out who owns the property you will need to find out where they are currently living. Any of the following website will help you in locating the owner's address and sometimes phone number.

publicrecords.searchsystems.net

knowx.com

Homeinfomax.com

Anywho.com

411. com

reversephonedirectory.com

Zabasearch.com

emailfinder.com

yellowpages.com

Propertyshark.com

Once you find the owner you need to contact them either by phone or by mail to see if they are interested in selling the property. If you wish to contact them by phone below is a Phone Script that I use when calling about a property. This script will make it easier for you to stay on track and ask the questions that you need to evaluate a property and see if it is a potential deal.

Sample phone script for a vacant property

My name is… I am calling about your vacant property located at…

Are you interested in selling this property?

Are you the owner?

May I ask your name?

Can you give me a little information about the property?

How many bedrooms, baths?

Does it have a basement?

How much are you asking for the property?

How did you come up with that figure?

Have you had it appraised?

How long has your home been vacant?

How long have you owned it?

Is it listed with a real estate agent?

Have you had any offers? Any written?

If I offered you all cash and could close in 30 days, what is the least you would take? ** PAUSE

When did you get your mortgage?

What is your mortgage balance?

Is it current?

Do you have any other mortgages?

Can we set up a time for me to see the property?

Expired MLS listings

I don't know about you but as a kid I always got stuck with the *"Hand me downs"*. I was the youngest child in the family and would always get the clothes that everyone else already wore. I would get the jeans that were already worn out, the shirts that had the color washed out etc...

I never really appreciated the concept of "Hand me downs" as a child. I mean who wants something that someone else has already worn out? Something that someone has already had in their possession for about 4 months before they decide it is of no use to them anymore. You know where I am going with this right?

Exactly!!! Expired listings are the real estate version of "Hand me downs". Check this out... A Realtor lists a property and puts it on the MLS. This is where it gets worn out, washed through and picked apart. Then one day the listing expires and the property is available for the picking. Just like an old shirt or an old pair of jeans. If it fits wear it!

The best thing is that these are sellers that have been trying to sell their house for whatever reason and are now more motivated than they were when they first listed their property. They may have fallen behind in their mortgage payments and tried to sell their house to prevent foreclosure. If this is the case than you now become a new hope to them and you get a chance to help someone out while making a profit. These are my favorite kind of properties because I can offer these sellers another chance to relieve their burden.

If you have a Realtor on your team have them send you all of the expired listings in a particular area that you have buyers in. Go through the listings and pull out the ones that say *"Motivated seller"*, *"Handy man"* or *"bring offers"*.

You can send them a letter stating your interest in purchasing the property. If they contact you in regards to your letter than ask them to tell you about the property. You can use the Sample Phone Script that I have included in this chapter.

Remember to do as much research as possible on the property before you go to look at it. This will help in your negotiations.

I now have a new respect for "hand me downs". I am now standing with my trash bag open shouting *"Put them in here!"*

Finding properties by searching the "for rent" ads.

Rental ads can also be ads placed by sellers who could not sell their property so they have decided to rent the property to keep up with the mortgage. Search online classifieds and your local paper for properties for rent. If the description does not state *"newly rehabbed"*, *"new paint and carpet"* etc… then it was probably not posted by an Investor, but rather a home owner who may need to sell but can't. This is not always the case but by not calling to find out you could be passing up a good property deal.

Call the number in the ad and ask if the property is also for sale. If so, get some details on the property including address, asking price etc… Tell the seller that you need to do some research on the property and will call them back shortly. Once you do your research and determine that it could be a good deal for you call them back and set up a time to take a look at the property.

Finding estate properties before they even reach probate

Estate properties make the best wholesale deals. Most of these properties are owned free and clear (no mortgage balance) and the family is usually motivated to sell to settle the estate.

In today's market we are witnessing a huge inventory of estate properties due to the 1946 Baby Boom. Post WWII, 9 months after all of the soldiers returned from war there were 3.4 million babies born. The largest number of babies born in a single year. Today these Baby Boomers are around 70 years old which is the age when people start wanting to downsize and are motivated to sell or some may have passed away leaving the property to a family member. Whatever the life situation they are facing there is generally a property involved.

Though it is difficult to locate these Baby Boomers while they are still alive it is not so difficult to reach out to the family once they have passed away. Often times the family is left the property and have no resources to keep up with the property. These properties usually need repair as they are out dated and therefore the family feels they cannot list the property with a Realtor until the repairs are done. While the family waits to get the funds together to update the property the property sits vacant deteriorating further. The family is left with the responsibility to keep up with the real estate taxes and maintain the property. This can be a huge burden for a family.

This is where you come in. You will be able to offer your service and buy the property or wholesale the property and relieve the family of this burden. I love dealing with estate properties. Even though it can be very emotional to deal with the family you are actually helping them through the process of settling the estate that they would not have otherwise known how to do.

They have no idea that there is help available unless you tell them. This is why mailing letters to the family of a recently deceased loved one is so effective. Not only could you end up with a great wholesale deal but you have the opportunity to help a family by purchasing their property and settling their estate.

There are several ways to reach out to the family members with your interest to buy the property. One way is to go to your local probate court and get a list of the estates that are currently in probate. Once you get this list you can mail a letter to the families stating your interest in the property.

However, since there are so many other wholesalers and buyers marketing to the Probate lists I like to try to contact the families before they even reach Probate. This method takes a bit more time to implement, but it has proven to be a more successful strategy at finding estate properties.

A few ways that I find estate properties

1. Search the obituaries in your local newspaper. Most newspapers now have websites that enable you to search the archives. I suggest that you search the archives and go back at least 3 months. The first 3 months are usually the hardest time for the family and the most emotional time to deal with a deceased loved ones estate. I have been there many times and therefore I do not like to bother the family during this time.

Once you search the obituaries and find the name of the recently deceased you can go to your local real estate tax office, or to their website if they have one, and search the name to see if they owned a property. If so, simply mail a letter to "the estate of…" at that address stating your interest in the property.

2. Search google for your local funeral homes. You can simply put "*funeral home (your town)*" into the search bar. This should bring up multiple funeral homes in your area. Go to the website link and click on "obituaries". The obituaries should come up by date. You then want to go back three months and begin searching your local tax records for the name of the deceased. You can then repeat the process above in number 1 and mail out the estate letter to the family.

Remember when dealing with estate properties you must have compassion and be genuine with your condolences. This is a very delicate time for the family and your compassion matters.

There is a copy of my Estate Letter located in the back of this book. You will also be able to edit and print a copy in MY WHOLESALIN VAULT. **You will be given access to the Vault soon, I promise.**

Tips on negotiating with the seller on FSBO (for sale by owner) properties

Negotiations are the focus point of any wholesale deal. This is the part that turns the property into a deal. Negotiating the price and terms of a property with the seller is where the whole deal gets packaged up and ready for the next level... the sale.

When you are about to negotiate the price and terms of the property with the seller follow these guidelines.

STAY IN CONTROL!

You have already run your numbers and know what your MAO (maximum allowable offer) is for the property. You either need to be at that number or you need to walk away from the deal.

DO NOT GET EMOTIONAL!

As a wholesaler you will come in contact with many sellers that are in desperate situations, are dealing with a job loss or health issue or even some that are very intimidating and come off very arrogant about what they are expecting to get out of the deal. Leave your emotions at home when dealing with sellers. If you get too involved in the drama you might agree to pay more than you intended to pay when you first started the conversation. This will leave you holding a wholesale deal that you cannot move to an end buyer.

HE WHO BIDS FIRST LOSES!

Never be the first one to make an offer on a property. Always ask the seller what they are looking to get for the property and let them give you the first number. If you offer first you could be offering more than what the seller was hoping to get for the property. If the seller was thinking they would sell the property for $40,000.00 and you offered $50,000.00 you just robbed yourself of an extra $10,000.00 profit!

ALWAYS BE UPFRONT ABOUT YOUR INTENTIONS!

If you plan on wholesaling the property let the seller know that you may not be the one they are going to settlement with. Explain to them that you work with many partners and that you are not always the one that they will meet at the closing table. I believe in being honest after all everything will be exposed at the closing table.

Finding the market value of a property

Finding the Market Value or "ARV" (After repair value) of an investment property is the first step in determining if it is a good deal.

When I present an investment property to one of my buyers the first things that they want to know is the ARV (After repair value). This is the most important fact in determining if the property is a deal.

Finding the market value of a property is the key factor in determining a deal. The MLS (Multiple Listing Service) is the most accurate way to find the value of a property but only licensed Realtors have access to the MLS. Fortunately there are many web sites that link directly to the MLS and they are free for anyone to use.

These sites will give you an estimated ARV of a property along with a list of comparable houses that have sold in the area. Below are links to some of the web sites that I have found most useful.

Totalviewrealestate.com

Zillow.com

Homevaluehunt.com

Homes.com

Homevalues.com

Homegain.com

Cyberhomes.com

Realestate.yahoo.com/homevalues

Try to use the estimates from a few different sites when you are looking at the market value of your property. Remember these sites only give you an estimated ARV, the only accurate ARV will come from your Agent.

Estimating the rehab costs of a property

As a Real Estate Wholesaler I must be able to effectively evaluate a property to ensure that it meets my buyer's criteria before I put the property under contract. This process of evaluation includes estimating the cost of renovating a property to bring it up to the retail market value (ARV) of the surrounding properties.

EVERYTHING WHOLESALING | Carol Stinson

When I look at a potential wholesale deal I must be able to estimate what it will cost to renovate the kitchen which is by far the most crucial factor of any retail sale. I must also consider the cost to replace the roof if needed, replace the windows if needed, estimate new floors and paint according to the sq. ft. of the property and so on...

This is a very important step in the wholesale process as my offer to the Seller depends mostly on this rehab cost estimate. I must deduct this cost from my initial offer to the Seller on the property to ensure that my buyer is still left with enough equity to make a profit after renovating the property.

So how does a wholesaler do this? If you know a contractor who will go in each property and give you a free estimate that is awesome. But honestly there are not many contractors that I know who will keep giving you free estimates on your properties without eventually wanting to get paid. Maybe you have some contracting knowledge so you are able to do your own repair estimates on your property leads or Uncle Tom is a contractor and for a six pack will give you estimates all day long. However this is not the case for many who are trying to wholesale properties to make a profit.

I have never been faced with the dilemma of not being able to effectively get a rehab estimate on a property due to the fact that my husband and my sons are all contractors and we own our own property renovation company in NJ. When I find a property then my boys or my husband will go with me to evaluate the rehab and all I have to do is give them dinner, works for me! But, even experienced contractors need a resource guide to renovation costs. They need to have a material price list, estimate labor costs and even demo and disposal costs. So how do they get these price?

I want to let you in on a little secret, a contractor's guide to renovation material and labor costs, a contractor's bible if you will. The **"RSMeans Contractor's Pricing Guide".** As a rehab company owner and being married to a contractor for over 28 years I can guarantee that 75% of contractors own this pricing guide!

This handy guide has everything a contractor needs to quickly and efficiently estimate rehab costs. This guide gives you the total unit price costs for every aspect of the most common repair and remodeling projects, in a format organized for the way you build from frame to finish. It covers every step needed to complete each task, and includes demolition, installation, painting, cleaning and more. It is so simple to understand and use that even those that are new to property renovations can quickly estimate the cost of any rehab. That means that even the newest Wholesaler can go through a property and figure out the price of a rehab so they can make an efficient offer on a property.

This Contractor's Pricing Guide is a must have for every wholesaler and real estate investor! It has never been easier to figure out the total repair costs to renovate a property. Even a novice wholesaler or real estate investor can literally figure out the renovation costs of a property in less than 30 minutes with this price guide. This guide is simple to use and gives you the cost of all materials from the nails all the way up to the larger materials needed for each project, the cost of labor and even the cost of demo and removal or materials. Seriously, how awesome is that?

If you're a wholesaler who is serious about giving your buyer the most efficient rehab estimate on a property or your just starting out in real estate investing or wholesaling than you will surly reap the benefits of having this price guide at your fingertips.

This Contractor's Pricing Guide is available on Amazon.com and in your local Home Depot or Lowes stores.

<u>Making an offer on a property</u>

I want to know quickly if a property is worth my time. I am not one for wasting my time on a property that will never become a deal and make me money. When I look at a property I want to know my MAO (Maximum allowable offer) before I even leave the property.

When you get a property lead the first thing any effective real estate wholesaler does is research the ARV. You want to know what that property will sell for after it's rehabbed before you even take the time to go look at it.

Once you know the ARV and feel confident that it's a real estate deal worth pursuing then the next thing to do is go look at the property to estimate the rehab.

I have wholesaled and estimated rehab costs on so many properties that when I walk through a property I can figure out the rehab in my head. But, not everyone is familiar with running rehab costs. A great guide to rehab costs is to multiply the sq. ft. of a property by 20 to get an estimated "basic' rehab costs. Ex. If I multiply a 1500 sq. Ft. house by 20 my estimated rehab cost would be $30,000.00 to do a basic rehab. A basic rehab is replacing the kitchen with basic materials (basic counter tops and appliances as opposed to granite and stainless steel), new bathroom fixtures, paint, carpet etc... This of course does not included replacing the roof, structural issues and other major repairs

So I run the following formula to get my MAO before I even leave the property. However, if you need to take notes as you walk through and then figure out the rehab you can run this formula when you're done.

Now that I know the ARV and have figured out the rehab costs I run the following formula to figure out my MAO (maximum allowable offer) to make an offer.

The magic offer formula

ARV x .70 – minus rehab costs – minus my wholesale fee x .97 = MAO

ARV (After Repair Value)

.70 (You're subtracting a 30% profit for your buyer)

Rehab costs (An estimate of cost of repairs)

Wholesale fee (The amount that you would like to make on the deal, your profit)

.97 (You're subtracting the 3% closing costs)

MAO (This is the maximum amount you can offer on the deal to make a wholesale profit)

Here is an example…

$100,000 x .70 – $10,000 – $5,000 x .97 = $53,350

This is a quick, easy wholesale formula that will guarantee that your deal is one that will sell and one that you will profit from.

Stay in control of every deal!

A good real estate wholesaler stays in control of their real estate deal at all times. From negotiations to sale it is very important that you stay in the driver's seat. What do I mean by this? Let's say that you have a real estate wholesale deal that you have negotiated and are ready to go meet with the seller and get the contracts signed. You made an appointment to meet with them in 2 days to get everything signed. You're anxious to get a sale on it so you send the information out to your wholesale buyers list to inform them about the deal. You go to your appointment and find out that the seller had already signed a contract with someone an hour earlier because they offered them $1,000 more than you did. Then you come to find out the person they just signed the contract with was on your wholesale buyers list. The seller had NO commitment with you, you marketed the real estate info to your buyers list before you had control or had the property under contract.

DO NOT market a wholesale property until you have a Purchase Agreement signed with the seller! Once you have a property under contract there are no more loop holes for someone to go through and cut you out. You have made the seller aware of the fact that your contract is a legal and binding contract between you and them. You can now fly a blimp over New York with the property information at this point as your deal with the seller is secure.

If it is a really good deal I suggest that you put the contract in an escrow account at a Title Company in an effort to cloud the title. If a property has a clouded title than no one can legally put out another contract on that property. I don't always do this. I only take the time to do this if the deal is really good and I stand to make a nice profit

If you feel that you must market that property before you get it under contract than I suggest that you X out the address when you market it. (Ex. 2xx Main St.) This way buyers have to call you to get the address. Just let these calls go to voice mail and call them back once you get the property under contract.

One more thing... do not let a buyer go to the property without you if it is owner occupied. I know you're thinking" I wouldn't do that". But, you would be surprised how many wholesalers send their buyers to a property without them because they just don't have the time to go. I guarantee you that buyer will be all over your seller asking all kinds of questions.

A Good wholesaler stays in control of their deals at all times. These little mistakes can cost you your profit and rob you of all of the time and effort you have put into making that deal happen.

Marketing a property

Now that you have found a property and negotiated a price with the seller you must let the world know that you have a property for sale. Below are some of the marketing resources that have been most productive for me in getting my properties sold.

Internet Resources

I take advantage of many of the free classified sites online. The internet is the largest real estate resource in the world. With both buyers and sellers turning to the internet for all of their real estate needs you want to make sure you have a great online presence when it comes to your local real estate market.

Below is a list of free online classified websites that I use. I suggest that you get familiar with them and use them to sell your properties and advertise for a buyer.

Byowner.com

Adpost.com

Sell.com

epage.com

Salespider.com

classifiedads.com

Stumblehere.com

Isell.com

Olx.com

Theflyer.com

Kugli.com

Epage.com

webclassifieds.com

Adpost.com

Oodle.com

Craigslist.com

Vflyer.com

Postlets.com

Backpage.com

Kilili.com

I use many of the online free classified sites and I find some of them to be more effective than others. For instance I am a big fan of postlets.com when it comes to marketing real estate properties that I am wholesaling. This resource is an awesome tool to have in your wholesale toolbox. When I get a real estate property under contract the first thing I do is create a POSTLET to help me market the property. With POSTLETS I am able to create a one page add about my property with pictures, information and a map and the best part is that it is a free resource. Not only does postlets.com enable me to create a presentation of my property but it does so much more.

You can copy the HTML code and post your wholesale property on craigslist. Doing this will give you a great presentation and description of your property to advertise on craigslist.

You can go down to the embedded code for your postlet minis. Copy any of the three embedded codes small, medium or large to put on your real estate or wholesale website.

Another great real estate wholesale tool is Vflyer.com. This tool is similar to postlets.com, but Vflyer has many more automatic submission sites. Your flyer will be automatically submitted to sites like OODLE, GOOGLE BASE, HOT PADS, CYBER HOMES, FRONT DOOR, TRULIA and ZILLOW. This gives you much more exposure for your real estate wholesale property.

** VFLYER tip… in the features section when you are creating a VFLYER it will ask you agents name and broker. Just put "NO AGENT" in agent section and "NO BROKER" in broker section. This ensures that your VFLYER is posted on sites like TRULIA and FRONT DOOR which is usually only available to agents and brokers. These sites get allot of buyer traffic and you don't want to miss out on it.

Craigslist.com has been my most successful online classified website. The best thing about craigslist is that you can narrow your marketing down to reach the buyers in your local market.

Bandit signs

Aside from internet marketing you can also market your property in your local area. Bandit signs are a good way to draw interest to your property and get buyers calling. I recommend not putting too much information on your bandit sign. The first reason is because too much information is hard to read when someone is driving down the road at 50 mph. The second reason is because you want to get them to call you or visit your website for the rest of the information. I simply put the number of bedrooms and price of the property with my phone number. This way the buyer needs to call me to get the address and rest of the information.

Flyers

Flyers are a great tool to advertise your property. I create a flyer of the property and mail it to my buyers as well as hang them up in a few of the area supermarkets. Flyers are an inexpensive way to advertise your property for sale and I have actually had some success with them.

Newspaper ads

Newspaper ads can be a very effective way to develop your buyers list when you advertise your property for sale. I generally advertise my property for sale in the local newspaper for thirty days. If the property is a really great deal I will let it run for an additional thirty days, even if it sells, to build my buyers list.

I suggest that you take advantage of both Internet and local marketing tools to get the best results. Marketing is the hub of your entire wholesaling career. It is the way that you find properties, find buyers and sell properties and it is the only way that you can successfully make money from home.

Chapter 4

BUYERS

One thing that I have learned in wholesaling is that there is a buyer for every property as long as the numbers leave a profit on the table. There is a buyer for every area in every market as long as there is a profit to be made. I have buyers in the suburbs and in the ghetto, buyers for single family properties and apartment buildings. Each buyer has their own criteria for what they buy and where they buy. All you have to do is have ONE great deal that matches ONE of their criteria and its money in the bank for you.

Most real estate wholesale training courses today start by teaching you to build your buyer's list first before you start making offers on properties. However, I like to compare finding buyers to fishing. I have found that though there are many ways to fish for buyers the best way to catch a fish is with good bait! You need to bait your hook with something the fish desire. Then you need to cast your line where the big fish swim. In other words you need a property (bait) to catch a buyer (big fish). Without the bait there is no logical reason for the fish to even consider your hook. Granted you can call the "*we buy houses*" numbers and tell them you get bait (properties) from time to time, but they will not take your hook seriously until it is baited. It's like standing at the foot of the lake saying " *here fishy fishy look what I have*" while shaking an empty hook. But, put some juicy bait on that hook and the buyers will be jumping at it.

Bottom line, the NUMBER ONE way to find buyers is with a great deal on your hook. I suggest that you are finding properties, making offers and building your buyers list simultaneously.

One thing that you can do while you're searching for properties is put "fake" bait on your hook to catch fish. When fishermen want to catch fish they bait their hook with rubber worms, slimy fake fish scented with some nasty oil stuff and even some lures. The fake bait must resemble real bait for the fish to bite. In real estate this "fake" bait is called a "GHOST AD". A ghost ad is an ad that you place on craigslist or in the newspaper that describes a property for sale. This property description is so enticing that it gets the buyer's calling for more information.

Using ghost adds

As I stated finding buyers is like fishing. When you go fishing you cannot just stand by the water and call out to the fish hoping they will come swimming to you to be caught. Reality, you must use bait to catch fish. The bigger and juicier the bait the more fish you will catch. The same goes for buyers. The better the bait (*description of a property for sale*) the more buyers you will catch. You must dangle this bait out there, move it around and then pull them in when they bite.

I have found that the #1 way to build a buyer's list is by using a "Ghost Ad". This could be a made up property deal or a great deal that you have had in the past. You can continue to use this deal over and over again to lure buyers. Look at it this way sometimes fishermen use rubber worms. A rubber worm that looks like a real worm is dangled in the water and the fish bite. Ghost ads are like rubber worms that look and smell like the real thing. Here are a few samples of ghost ads that may work for you:

Sample ghost adds

#1 Ugly House for sale

Handyman Special! 3 bedroom ranch on large lot in great area. Newer systems and roof but property needs cosmetic rehab.

Asking ... *(Every market is different so you need to put in a good wholesale price for your area)* serious cash buyer only!

#2 Estate Sale, MUST SELL!

Must sell to settle estate. 3 bedroom, 2 bath single home on large lot. Great area and schools. Property needs updating and repairs. Asking .... *(Every market is different so you need to put in a good wholesale price for your area)* Serious Cash Buyers only!

#3 Handy man special!

3 bedroom 1 bath in great area. She is UGLY and Needs rehab. Systems are good, foundation is good needs cosmetic rehab. Asking ... *(Every market is different so you need to put in a good wholesale price for your area)*. Serious cash buyers only!

I suggest that you run these ads in your local market on craigslist, in your local newspaper etc... When buyers call, and they will call, let them go to your voicemail. This way you automatically get their name and number and can add them to your buyer's list. When you call them back explain to them that this particular property is no longer available, but you have a few others. Ask for their email address so you can send them the details. Then when you do get a great property deal you can simply email them the details.

You should switch the wording of your ads, change the property description a bit, and advertise them every week on craigslist and in your local paper. This will continuously bring in buyers to add to your buyer's list. When you do get an actual property under contract you can do the same advertising with that property.

Bird dogging for investors

Bird Dogging is the process of locating properties for Investors without actually putting the property under contract as you do with Real Estate Wholesaling. There are many real estate investors that will pay up to $1,000 per lead. You get paid if you present the Investor with a property lead and they purchase the property. You only get paid if the property is purchased by them or one of their partners so make sure you make your property lead stand out. I will show you how to do research and get as much information as you can about a property before presenting it to a buyer in the upcoming chapters. Find out as much as you can about the property and remember there are allot of people giving them leads so you must make sure your lead stands out. The more information you give them the faster your lead moves to the top of the list.

To find Investors that pay for these leads call various leads in your local newspaper and check online for ads that say "I buy houses", "Cash for Houses" etc…. Then call them up and ask if they pay a finder's fee if you find them a property.

10 tips to building your buyer's list

Below are ten ways that you can successfully build a buyer's list.

1. Call ads that say "I buy houses" in the newspaper and also search google.com to find buyers in your area. Type in "I buy houses (your state)". This will pull up websites of Investors in your area.

2. Call about houses listed for rent in your local newspaper and on craigslist. Sometimes these are Investors that are looking to rent their properties.

3. Visit Investment groups in your area.

4. Put an ad in the newspaper or craigslist that states that you have properties 30%-50% below retail and you are looking for buyers.

5. Search your phone book for Real Estate LLCs or Investment companies.

6. Call builders and contractors in your area to see if they purchase rehab properties. You can also send them a letter that informs them that you have rehab properties that you are looking to sell and wanted to see if they are interested.

7. Join online investment groups. This is a great way to find real estate investors and wholesalers.

Biggerpockets.com

Realestate.com

realestateinvestor.com

realestatedealmakers.com

Thenaked-onvestor.com

8. Send a letter to the owner of a duplex or a triplex in your area. The owners are generally real estate investors. Simply tell them that you often come across deeply discounted multi-unit properties in your area and you were contacting Investors in the area to see if they would be interested in being contacted when you have a property for sale. GET CREATIVE!

9. Run a "Ghost Ad" (a made up house for sale.) in the newspaper or on craigslist that says 3 bedroom Handyman house for sale, motivated seller, MUST SELL!! (Put your area). This will get real estate investors calling and then you can just tell them that that property is no longer available. Ask them if you can contact them when you have another one for sale.

10. Join real estate investment groups on Facebook. There are literally hundreds of groups that are directed toward Real Estate Investors and wholesalers. Go through the members of the group and start adding them as friends. Then when you have a property for sale simply post it on your FB wall. Those that are in your area will reply.

The buyers list is the foundation that successful wholesaling is built on and every good wholesaler spends allot of time and energy building that list. Building your buyers list must be an ongoing process if you are ever going to be successful.

Recruiting buyers from the "for rent" ads

You can build your wholesale buyers list and find motivated sellers by calling the real estate for rent ads.

With real estate prices being lower than they ever have real estate investors are taking advantage of the great bargains and purchasing properties at great discounts and holding them until the market improves. Once the market improves and housing prices go back up these Investors will sell these properties and make a huge profit. Since these investors are going to buy and hold these properties they must rent them out to cover their holding cost. They will buy, rehab and then advertise the property for rent. It is easy to spot an

Investor's "for rent" ad as it will state "newly rehabbed" or "new paint and carpet" etc… If the ad mentions that the property has been recently rehabbed it is safe to assume that this is a buy and hold buyer renting out their newly purchased property.

I suggest that you call these for rent ads that mention that the property has been recently renovated and ask the person that posted the ad if they are looking for more properties. If so get their information and add them to your buyer's list.

So next time your browsing through the for rent adds, stop and make the call. It could prove to be a diamond in the ruff!

Recruiting speculative buyers

Since the mortgage crisis of 2009 produced an unprecedented number of foreclosures across the country, Investors were able to scoop up discounted inventory and many took advantage of foreclosures and short sales.

This wave of real estate activity enabled the real estate market to slowly rebound as these discounted properties were rehabbed and flipped at market prices.

During 2012 to 2014 – this rebound effect drove the recovery. Now, though, the rebound effect is fading. Property price levels and price changes are both approaching normal and foreclosure inventories are dwindling. This is inevitable as the market improves and therefore shifts to price increases and a healthier mix of home sales. With housing prices increasing, real estate Investors are now finding it hard to find flip inventory that will produce a quick return on their investment. As a result, this lack of flip inventory has made way for a new pool of real estate Investors to begin to drive the real estate market, "Speculative buyers".

Speculative investment: to speculate, to anticipate a great return.

Speculative buyers will purchase a property with the intent of holding the property (*renting it out*) until the market prices fully rebound and then sell the property for top dollar. Speculative investing works best when a market is positioned at the rebound stages of a seller's market. After a market goes through a buyer's market phase and the market is transitioning to a seller's market this will provide the upswing necessary to capitalize on as speculation. When the market is positioned correctly, the speculator has the best chance of capitalizing big-time on a speculative investment.

These speculative investments can come in many forms and all of them are betting on one primary objective. Buy a property at a low price with the anticipation of selling when the market fully rebounds for top dollar. Speculative Investors will generally purchase a property with cash, do some rehab and place a tenant in the property. They will then do a cash out refinance, pulling their cash back out, and hold the property until the market reaches a point of high return.

The next stage in the housing recovery depends on fundamentals such as job growth, rising incomes, and more household formation. Importantly, the share of young adults with jobs is still less than halfway back to normal, many young adults are still living with their parents, and income growth is sluggish. This means that housing activity in 2015 might disappoint by some measures. Since many young adults today are currently carrying a large amount of student loans, qualifying for a mortgage is near impossible. Therefore today's young adults along with those who have lost their home in the recent foreclosure crisis, have caused the rental market to explode. Since the demand in rental properties is higher than the supply, the rental market will remain vigorous for years to come.

Since Speculative Buyers are willing to pay a bit more for their Investments it should be easier for real estate wholesalers to find properties. Many wholesalers have been experiencing a shortage of inventory as the sellers are not accepting offers low enough for a wholesaling spread. Much of this resistance to low offers is the result of the mortgage balance on a property being the same as or over the market value of the property. This does not leave much room for negotiating the price. But, with speculative buyers willing to pay a bit more for a property *(because they will be able to reap a nice cash flow with the booming rental market)* wholesalers can increase their offers on properties resulting in a higher success rate of accepted offers.

The key to successful wholesaling in today's market is to recruit more speculative buyers. This will enable you to increase your offers resulting in a higher influx of wholesale properties.

When to ask your buyer for a POF (proof of funds)

As you build your Buyer's List you are going to be adding buyers that are genuine and buyers that are simply tire kicking. It's just the way it is. I have a buyers list of over 7,000 buyers across the Country and when I tell you that only about 70% of them are actually buyers I am not exaggerating. The truth is that maybe 25% out of the 70% actually buy from me. This is why it is so important to continually build your buyer's list as you need to increase the number of actually buyers on your list.

Many if not most of your buyers on your list will consist of wholesalers looking to flip your property over to one of their buyers. But that's ok, I keep wholesalers on my list because wholesalers have buyers so in essence I am adding genuine buyers to my list through them.

Never ask a new buyer to show proof that he can buy (POF Proof of funds) before he shows interest in a particular property as you can discourage him from working with you. Most people do not appreciate baring their assets to others unless they are really serious about buying a particular property. So having them show proof prematurely can be a turn off for them. I suggest that you simply keep adding buyers to your list and only proof their funds when they are ready to purchase one of your properties.

One way to see if a buyer is genuine is to search your County tax records website for their name or the name of their LLC. Many County tax records are now available online so call your County Tax office and ask for their website or do a google search for tax records in your County. When you put their name into the website it will bring up all of their properties that they own in a particular County. Genuine buyers will usually own several pieces of real estate. This is a great way to see if a certain buyer on your list is an actual buyer.

I only use the tax records to give me a general feel for a buyer. If a buyer looks at one of my properties and wants to go to contract to purchase the property I will ask for a POF or Proof of funds from them. This POF needs to come directly from their bank that proves that he has the funds to purchase the property. Once he supplies this POF I will call the bank listed on the POF to verify the funds. The bank cannot tell you how much is in the account but they can tell you if the buyer has enough in the account to cover the purchase of the property.

I always wait until a buyer is interested in purchasing one of my properties before I ask for a POF. If he cannot proof up I will not move forward with the contract. I do not want to hold up one of my properties with a buyer who cannot perform. If I allow a buyer to put my property under contract without proving that he can buy it puts me at risk of not selling the property to another buyer before my contract with the seller runs out.

The importance of networking

If you want to succeed in Wholesaling you have got to make some noise, rattle some cages and let the world know who you are. A Wholesaler that simply sits in his little neck of the woods holding his contracts in his hands excited about the deals that he has locked up will never sell a single one if he doesn't network. Networking with investors and other wholesalers in your area is what is going to get your deals sold and money in your pocket. If you are not networking you are not going to make money. It's that simple.

The first network that you want to tap into is the one right in your back yard. Find Investor Groups in your area and go to a meeting. Introduce yourself, give out business cards and even hand out info on your deals. Visit reiclub.com or meetup.com to locate an Investor group near you.

Next you should begin networking with buyers via Social Media.

facebook.com

Twitter.com

Linkedin.com

Now it is time to join the Investor Forums. These forums with both get you networking with Investors and build your knowledge of Wholesaling. Most of these groups have articles and online education available.

Biggerpockets.com

Realestate.com

realestateinvestor.com

meetup.com

There are hundreds of social networks out there. I would suggest that you create a profile and add your contact number in each forum. I have found many buyers in these forums and have found them to be a very valuable asset to my success as a Wholesaler and an Investor.

Bottom line… There has never been a better time than now to profit from real estate. With foreclosures, pre-foreclosures, short sales and REO properties there is a flood of opportunity to buy houses at a huge discount. There is no doubt that there are more discounted properties than there are buyers for these properties. There are Investors and Corporations that are ready, willing and able to buy these properties and there are huge profits to be made in putting the two together.

Whether you want to find properties for Investors (Bird dogging), assign properties to end buyers (Wholesaling) or invest yourself there has never been a larger window of opportunity.

Chapter 5

CREATIVE WHOLESALING

There are times when traditional wholesaling methods will not be effective in wholesaling a property. It is times like these when a Wholesaler must get creative to get the deal closed and make a profit.

I remember when I started in Real Estate back in 2008, the market was prime for wholesaling. I found vacant properties located the owner of the property and negotiated a purchase price. The property owners were not upside down on their mortgage (owing more on their mortgage balance than the property was worth) and the property was usually vacant due to the loss of a loved one etc...

Those days are over! In today's market the massive inventory of vacant properties are the result of the Sub Prime Mortgage crisis that began in 2008. Sub Prime Mortgages were given to home buyers in 2006 and 2007 in an effort for the banks to supply the huge demand of Mortgage Backed Securities to Wall Street Investors.

These Sub Prime Mortgages were given to home buyers with poor credit and those who did not financially qualify could provide stated income verification. As a result of the higher credit risk the home buyer received an adjustable interest rate that would start out at a high 11% and would reset in the future to a higher 14%.. This meant that these Mortgage Backed Securities offered Investors a high rate of return due to the higher interest rates on the mortgages. However, those high adjustable rates ultimately caused massive defaults when the interest rates began to reset to a higher rate in 2008. Once this happened the home owner found it difficult to afford the higher interest rate payment resulting in major defaults and massive foreclosures. These foreclosed properties now take up the majority of the inventory of properties for sale in real estate markets around the Country.

There are some who say that we are currently seeing a "housing recovery". They believe that the market is stabilizing and that the housing market is going to start the incline to higher housing prices. According to the 2013 CoreLogic' National Foreclosure Report An analysis shows 52,000 foreclosures were completed in May 2013, a 27 percent year-over-year decline from 71,000 in May

2012. Completed foreclosures are an indication of the total number of homes actually lost to foreclosure.

"We continue to see a sharp drop in foreclosures around the country and with it a decrease in the size of the shadow inventory. Affordability, despite the rise in home prices over the past year, and consumer confidence are big contributors to these positive trends. We are particularly encouraged by the broad-based nature of the housing market recovery so far in 2013." ~ Anand Nallathambi, president and CEO of CoreLogic.

This statistic is based on foreclosures **"completed"**, those properties that have completed the foreclosure process and are now Bank Owned Properties or REOs. This statistic does not take into consideration the thousands of foreclosures that are backlogged in the courts of judicial foreclosure states. These properties have not yet been completed and in some states will not be completed for several years.

FLORIDA currently has a logjam of 14,471 pending defaults that continues to stagnate the court system, and more than one third of the cases dismissed this year were dismissed without a judgment. As a result, those foreclosures could still circle back into the courts when lenders eventually produce the paperwork or make other necessary adjustments, according to an update released from the State Courts Administrator.

NEW JERSEY currently has a large backlog of distressed homes that piled up while the mortgage industry dealt with accusations that homeowners' rights were being abused in the foreclosure process. The average number of days a mortgage is in foreclosure from the notice of default to completion stood at 1072 days in New York and more than 900 days in New Jersey, according to *RealtyTrac.*

About half of the 50 states have judicial foreclosure systems. The housing market crash so bogged down the systems in New York and New Jersey that foreclosures there have routinely dragged on for two or three years; their timelines are among the longest in the country. The national average, which factors in non-judicial states, is about one year, according to RealtyTrac, which monitors foreclosures nationwide.

I can go on and on but I think you get the point. Don't believe the HYPE about an end to the foreclosure crisis being on the horizon. The truth is that in many states the harvest of foreclosed properties is just about to start. As the foreclosure backlog is cleared in judicial states it will open the flood gates for a substantial number of REO properties. Once the Courts begin to clear some of these foreclosures, like a clogged pipe, they will begin to flood the market creating a harvest of REO properties.

The number of foreclosures that are sitting in a backlog has the ability to create a bountiful harvest for wholesalers. If it will take an average of 900 days for these foreclosures to become "completed" that means that those foreclosures that are in the front of the line are about to hit the market and the properties that just entered the foreclosure process will hit in about 900 days. This creates a HUGE backlog that will slowly flow into the wholesale harvest for another 3 years or so. Wholesalers need to step up their game and be prepared to wholesale these properties. Unless the Wholesaler gets creative in closing these deals they will miss the pending opportunity to reap in this harvest. Making offers and finding buyers is one thing, confidently closing them is another. Learning how to get these deals closing is imperative to your survival as a Wholesaler in today's real estate market.

Deed restrictions and anti- assignment clauses

One of the stumbling blocks wholesalers run into when trying to wholesale these properties are the anti- assignment clauses and deed restrictions set by the banks when purchasing a Foreclosures, REO or Short Sale property.

Sample "No assignment" clause": *Purchaser shall not assign its rights or obligations under this agreement to another party, without the prior written approval of the other party.*

Sample deed restriction on a cash transaction: *The Grantee(s), or purchaser(s), of the Property may not re-sell, record an additional conveyance document, or otherwise transfer title to the Property within 60 days following the execution of this Deed.*

These deed restrictions and non- assignment clauses have hindered many wholesalers from wholesaling one of these properties to their buyer. Therefore most Wholesalers are stuck when it comes to closing these properties and making a profit.

The truth is that a Wholesaler is basically a "Transaction Engineer" able to engineer a closing transaction in a way that will allow them to profit at closing. Since contracts are what we sell to our buyers (Not properties as only Agents can sell properties) we must be "Contract Magicians" able to create an effective contract so that we can get paid at closing. We must be creative, while obeying contract law, in various transactions that can transfer a property from seller to buyer. There is more than one way to transfer properties and being familiar will all of the methods used to transfer properties and getting creative is the key to effective wholesaling.

When utilizing creative wholesaling methods you must make sure that your closing method remains within the guidelines of what is legal and ethical. In the following chapters you are going to learn legally creative strategies that I use to quickly and easily transfer foreclosure properties over to my buyers. Some of the strategies that I am about to cover you may have never thought of and a few you may have heard of but never knew how to put them in play in your wholesale deals. I am going to not only take you step by step in how to implement these methods but also the contracts needed to implement each strategy can be found at the back of the book and in MY WHOLESALING VAULT.

Wholesaling short sales

Though they can take months to complete, short sales are effective in creating an equity spread that will provide a nice profit to the wholesaler. The process of negotiating with the banks to take a purchase price that is lower than the amount owed on the loan is often the only way to create equity on a property. In a market dominated by REO properties being sold at discounted prices the ARV (After Repair Value) of the surrounding properties is often much lower than the mortgage balances owed by the owners of those properties. This strips the property of any equity and makes it impossible to sell the property since the value is lower than the mortgage balance. When there is negative equity in a property the only option is to present a short sale offer to the bank asking them to consider taking less than the mortgage amount that is owed on the property. In order for the bank to consider a short sale the homeowner must be behind on mortgage payments and provide details of the financial hardship that led to the missed mortgage payments.

A few examples of hardship are...

1. Unemployment / reduced income
2. Divorce
3. Medical emergency
4. Job transfer out of town
5. Bankruptcy
6. Death

Once the financial package is prepared and the purchase agreement is signed between the buyer and the seller (remember the seller is still the home owner at this point) the entire package is submitted to the bank. This is where the waiting period begins. It could takes up to 6 months to get a short sale approved so patience is needed when using this method to get property discounts. If the bank feels that it is in their best interest to sell the property at a discounted price they will approve the short sale offer and sell the property to you.

Since the banks will not allow you to assign the contract and the deed restrictions prevent you from doing a double close to transfer the property to your buyer then... what do you do? By including the following wording in your contract you will be able to wholesale the deal once it is approved:

Using "and/ or Nominee

On the Purchase Agreement write your name as buyer and next to your name write "*and/ or Nominee*". When you endorse the Purchase Agreement write "*and/ or Nominee*" next to your signature.

In the "Remarks" section of the Purchase Agreement place the following statement... "*Buyer reserves the right to register the property in another name or entity.*"

Explain to the Agent that since Short Sales take a few months to process and you will be actively buying other investment properties during that time you want to have the opportunity to pull in a partner if needed when the time comes to close the property. Explain that often times the partner is your money lender and they generally want to be on title to protect their interest in the loan This will allow you to replace your name as stated on the Purchase Contract with your Partner/ buyer's name for closing. When you find a buyer/ partner the Agent needs to draw up an Amendment to the Purchase Agreement that changes the name of the purchasing entity (your buyer/ partner) to be registered on the deed at closing. The Amendment will require your signature as well as your buyer's signature. Once the Amendment is fully endorsed you will forfeit your position as buyer and your buyer now steps into this position. You collect your fee upon the endorsement of the Amendment by both you and your buyer.

You are not doing anything illegal as you are laying out your intentions from the start by stating that you may be taking title to the property in the name of another entity. Allot can change in someone's financial situation while waiting for the short sale approval. Especially if it takes 6 months or more for an approval. You want to ensure that you can close the deal with someone else should your financial situation fall short when the time comes to close the deal. Many of my Private Lenders require either first position note and mortgage on the property or their name on Title to the property. Therefore I generally put and/ or Nominee on all of my short sale contracts just in case I get a lender on board that requires their entity be on Title. This saves me the hassle of trying to switch out the buyer's name later when it's time to close.

The following strategy is also effective in closing Short Sales.

Wholesaling foreclosure & REO properties

There is nothing more frustrating to a Wholesaler than finding an REO, negotiating the price, finding a buyer and then not being able to close on the property because of a deed restriction, assignment clause. In today's market the banks have placed deed restrictions on all of their Foreclosures, REOs and Short Sale properties. This deed restriction prevents the buyer from transferring ownership of the property to another entity for 30, 60 or 90 days depending on the specific deed restriction. As I stated earlier this means that a double close on a wholesale deal is not going to happen with a deed restriction in place. But honestly the banks are not going to hunt you down if you were to sell the property before the end of the deed restriction. There are no deed restriction police guarding public records in your local court house and there is no deed restriction jail to throw you in. But, the title company or closing entity WILL NOT allow you to double close on a property with a deed restriction in place.

Before we go any further I would first like to clarify the difference between a Foreclosure and an REO property.

The difference between a foreclosure and an REO

Foreclosure is where the bank takes possession of the property because of non-payment for a long period of time or an unapproved short sale. Another example would be a "Deed in lieu of foreclosure", a deed instrument in which a mortgagor (i.e. the borrower) conveys all interest in a real property to the mortgagee (i.e. the lender) to satisfy a loan that is in default and avoid foreclosure proceedings.

An REO is a bank-owned property ("real-estate owned"), when homes go into foreclosure they are sold at a trustee sale, if no one purchases it at the trustee sale, they become REO properties. Later they are often listed by Realtors hired by the bank."

Many times you can get a greater discount for a Foreclosure property as opposed to an REO because the foreclosing entity saved the expense of the foreclosure process, court fees, Attorney fees etc... The Judicial process of taking a property through the Court to foreclose can cost the foreclosing entity an estimated $30,000.00 just to complete the process. This added expense must be accounted for in the end sale of the property thus creating a higher purchase price for the property.

A Foreclosure Process is a specific legal process in which a lender attempts to recover the balance of a loan from a borrower who has stopped making payments to the lender by forcing the sale of the asset used as the collateral for the loan. There are two types of foreclosures, Judicial and Non- Judicial.

Judicial Foreclosure - *Foreclosure by judicial sale*, more commonly known as *judicial foreclosure*, which is available in every state (and required in many), involves the sale of the mortgaged property under the supervision of a court, with the proceeds going first to satisfy the mortgage; then other lien holders; and, finally, the mortgagor/borrower if any proceeds are left.

JUDICIAL FORECLOSURE STATES

Connecticut

Delaware

Florida

Illinois

Indiana

Kansas

Kentucky

Louisiana

Maine

Maryland

Massachusetts

Nebraska

New Jersey

New Mexico

New York

North Dakota

Ohio

Oklahoma

Pennsylvania

South Carolina

South Dakota

Vermont

Wisconsin

Oklahoma, South Dakota and Wisconsin have non-judicial foreclosure provisions in their state laws; however, judicial foreclosure is common.

Non Judicial Foreclosure - This process involves the sale of the property by the mortgage holder without court supervision. In judicial sale, the mortgage holder and other lien holders are respectively first and second claimants to the proceeds from the sale. This process is faster and cheaper for the Mortgagee.

NON-JUDICIAL FORECLOSURE STATES

Alabama

Alaska

Arizona

Arkansas

California

Colorado

District of Columbia

Georgia

Hawaii

Iowa

Michigan

Minnesota

Mississippi

Missouri

Montana

Nevada

New Hampshire

North Carolina

Oregon

Rhode Island

Tennessee

Texas

Utah

Virginia

Washington

West Virginia

Wyoming

Some non-judicial foreclosure states are handled as trustee sales.

As you can see there is a difference in a foreclosure and an REO property however that does not affect the deed restrictions or non-assignment clauses as the bank sets these rules as far as how these properties can be purchased and transferred.

The following techniques can be used to transfer your equitable interest in a property to a buyer for a profit without violating the contractual non- assignment clause and without having the extra closing costs to double close. By utilizing the following techniques when closing on Foreclosure, REO and Short Sale properties you will also not be violating the contractual deed restriction. The same entity that closed on the property remains on the recorded property deed throughout the 30, 60 or 90 day deed restriction put in place by the bank. The best part is that you reap your profit in the process!

Selling the LLC

The following strategy will require that you create an LLC that will be utilized for the sole purpose of transferring your equitable rights to a property from you to your buyer. You will be selling your membership/ownership in the LLC to your end buyer in exchange for your wholesale fee .This LLC will not be used for any other business transactions and must stay free from any activity other than the purpose it was created for.

There is a fee involved in creating an LLC however there is only one transaction taking place, closing on the property, so you will only have one set of closing costs to deal with. Therefore the fee for creating an LLC is much lower than the fees involved in a double close. So if you calculate the costs of each it is less expensive to create an LLC and transfer it over to your buyer.

I create all of my LLCs at Legalzoom.com as they are very inexpensive and you receive your LLC paperwork quickly.

THE PROCESS

1. Pick a name for the LLC. Something simple like "A" Property LLC" would do. Then once you sell that one you can create "B Property LLC" and so on....

2. List yourself as the ONLY member of the LLC. This makes it much easier since there are no other members to consult when you are ready to sell the LLC.

3. When you form the LLC the Operating Agreement should define the management structure of the company, and allow for the transfer of management rights.

4. Begin making offers in the name of the newly created LLC.

Once you get an offer accepted and the Purchase Agreement is drafted you will endorse the purchase contract by placing "*and/or membership Nominee*" next to your signature. This way you are giving full disclosure of your intentions. If you are questioned on this simply state that many times your private money lender requires that their interest in the property be protected through membership shares in the LLC.

When you get an interested buyer be sure to inform them that you will be transferring your property interest to them by selling the newly formed LLC. Assure them that the LLC was created solely for the purpose of selling it and that there are no liens or debts incurred in the LLC. They will most likely want to run a search on the LLC and check the standing of the LLC Entity on their own.

You transfer your interest in the property to your buyer by selling the LLC either before closing or at closing depending on what the buyer feels comfortable with.

Selling the LLC before closing

You and the buyer endorse the LLC sale contract and get it notarized before closing. You receive your fee and the buyer now becomes the managing member of the LLC and closes on the property.

Selling the LLC at closing

At closing the buyer funds the deal and you close on the property as the buyer and sign all of the contracts. While you are still at the closing table for the property the *"Sale of LLC Interest"* contract is endorsed and notarized by you and the buyer and you are paid your fee. Some buyers prefer to buy the LLC at the closing table to ensure that the property closes before they pay you your fee.

The buyer will need to send this fully endorsed and notarized contract to the state and register their name as the new owner of the LLC.

Transferring LLC membership interest

Selling membership interest in the LLC is another way to transfer your interest in the property to your buyer. You will still need to place *"and/or membership Nominee"* next to your signature on the Purchase Agreement to disclose your intentions.

There are some banks that may require that you sign the closing documents since you were the original signer on the Purchase Contract for the property. Therefore you will need to retain a portion of the LLC membership so that you can sign at closing. If this is the case then you can simply sell off 99% of the LLC membership to your buyer and retain 1% membership interest enabling you to sign the closing documents. 1% ownership of an LLC is almost no interest at all but it will enable you to sign on behalf of the LLC at closing. Your buyer will actually own 99% of the LLC which is basically full ownership.

The sale of membership interests must be done prior to closing. Then once you close on the property you can sell the remaining 1% interest in the property to your buyer via the "Sale of LLC Interest" contract and receive your fee. I do this right at the closing table immediately following the closing of the property. By you maintaining 1% interest in the LLC the buyer would not be able to sell the property in the future without your permission. Therefore it is in the best interest of the buyer to buy you out 100%. It is also in your best interest to sell him the remaining 1% interest so you can get paid. This is the incentive that both of you will have to get this done immediately after closing on the property.

A membership sale transfer does not need to be recorded with the state as you are still a 1% member of the LLC and the LLC itself has not changed ownership. The membership interests in an LLC can be sold according to the rules of your operating agreement. Make sure you retain a copy of all the documentation associated with the transaction as well as your buyer.

Once you receive your fee and after closing is complete on the property you can transfer the 1% ownership over to your buyer. If you transfer 100% of the ownership over to your buyer this will have to be recorded with the state via a *"Sale of LLC Interest"* contract.

Using a land trust to close foreclosures, REOs and short sales

I saved the best strategy for last! Using a land trust for your REO wholesale deals is by far the best, most effective way to transfer your interest in a property over to your buyer!

Land trusts are a great way to assign a property over to a buyer when closing on a foreclosure or REO property. A land trust is a revocable, living trust used specifically for holding title to real estate. The ownership of a land trust (referred to as "beneficial interest") is assignable. Once property is titled into the trust, the beneficiary of the trust can be changed without changing title to the property. This is great news when a real estate contract is non-assignable, such as in the case of a Short Sale, foreclosure or REO property. Instead of making your offer in your own name, make the offer in the name of a land trust, then assign your interest in the land trust to a third party.

What is a land trust?

A land trust is a simple, inexpensive method for handling the ownership of real estate. It is an arrangement by which the recorded title to the real estate is held by a trustee, but all the rights and conveniences of ownership are exercised by the beneficial owner (beneficiary) whose interest is not disclosed. This method of owning real estate eliminates many of the difficulties that otherwise may be encountered in acquiring, owning, or selling real estate.

The beneficiary of a land trust changes his or her interest in the property from real estate (title to the property) to personal property (ownership of the beneficial interest). Even though the beneficiary retains complete management and control over the property itself, he or she is not burdened with the legal characteristics of real estate when he or she deals with the property.

Since the beneficial interest is considered to be personal property, it is treated in much the same manner as a car, a savings account, or other tangible property. Consequently, the beneficial interest can be sold, pledged, or assigned in a simpler fashion than a conveyance of realty.

How does a land trust operate?

A land trust may be created by anyone capable of entering into a contract—an individual; a group of persons such as a partnership, syndicate, or business association; or two or more private individuals who desire to purchase and own the real estate as a joint venture.

Under a land trust agreement, the beneficiary retains complete control of the real estate in the same manner as if the recorded title were in his or her name. He or she may end the trust whenever desired and may add additional property to the trust at any time. At all times the beneficiary deals with the property as though he or she were the record title owner, for, as a matter of fact, he or she *is* the owner. The trustee executes deeds and mortgages and deals with the property only if directed in writing by the beneficiary.

When title to real estate is held in a land trust, the interest of the beneficiary, under terms of the trust agreement, is personal property. Since the beneficiary's interest is personal property, he or she may transfer it by assigning that interest without the formality of executing and acknowledging a deed; the wife or husband need not join in such assignment for the purpose of releasing the spouse's homestead rights.

What are the benefits of a land trust?

There are many benefits derived from the use of a land trust.

1. Privacy of Ownership.

Under a land trust, the identity of the real owner is never disclosed to the public. This feature can be important for many reasons. For example, a number of persons may be purchasing several parcels of real estate for some special purpose, and it may be that the desired result can be best accomplished if the objective is not made public; co-owners may desire that the interest of each member must be kept confidential; or an individual owner may not want to be burdened. Whatever the reason may be for not disclosing the identity of the real owner, a land trust provides the answer. Of course, certain governmental agencies and others, following valid and authorized legal processes, can ask about the beneficial ownership.

2. Protection for the owner.

A land trust offers particular benefits in those cases where the real estate is held by two or more persons. If the property is owned by two or more persons, the title to the property might become faulty and un-merchantable because of death, legal disability, divorce, judgments, and many other types of litigation affecting one of the co-owners. When the property is held in a land trust, a judgment against one of the beneficiaries does not constitute a lien upon the real estate held in trust; neither do the ordinary legal proceedings against any of the beneficiaries muddle the title.

Although the real estate itself is not encumbered by a judgment lien, the interest of the beneficiary in a land trust can be subject to the claims of creditors. If the title to the real estate is in the name of a trustee, the creditors must take additional steps to assert claims against the property.

3. Succession and ownership.

It has been a common practice to create joint tenancy in real estate holdings solely for the purpose of providing a succession of ownership upon death without the expense and delay of probate proceedings. Under joint ownership, however, either of the joint tenants is given an immediate interest in the ownership and management of that property, and in many cases, it handicaps the real owner as he or she cannot deal with the property without the written consent of the joint owner and the other spouse.

Under a land trust agreement, the party creating the trust can retain sole control over the property during his or her lifetime, with the desired succession in ownership becoming effective upon death without, under certain conditions, the expense of going through probate proceedings. This can be especially helpful to those who live out of state but own real estate in this state. They will not need to institute separate probate proceedings here but can have the land trust property administered in their home states.

4. Ease of conveyance.

A land trust affords a convenient means of mortgaging and selling a trust property without having to obtain deeds from all the beneficiaries and their spouses. It dispenses with the necessity of obtaining the release and waiver of homestead from the spouses of the parties interested in the trust real estate. These are noteworthy features if many individuals are interested in the property and are scattered throughout the United States.

Also since the beneficial interest is considered to have the legal characteristics of personal property, it can be pledged for a loan according to the same standards as stocks, bonds, automobiles, or other personal property without the restrictions and formalities of mortgages, title reports, and policies. Such assignments, although substantially easier than conveyances of realty, can produce a gift and transfer tax consequences.

5. Disposing of part interest.

A land trust simplifies the practical problem of disposing of a part interest in a property since the beneficial interest under a land trust can be transferred by assignment; no deed is needed. This process avoids a deed's formal requirements concerning acknowledgment, recording, and joinder by the grantor's spouse, although it may trigger a transfer tax. This aspect of the adaptability of a land trust becomes important when real estate is held by a number of persons, such as a group of heirs, or if the owners have disproportionate shares of the property.

The process of assigning a land trust

1. Create a Land Trust.

2. Create a Land Trust. You can use the "Trust Agreement" located at the back of the book or ask your Attorney to draw up a Trust Agreement for you.

3. Name your Land Trust something generic like "2015 1 TRANSACTION TRUST"

4. List yourself as Trustee.

5. Make offers in the name of your Land Trust and sign your name as Trustee of the Trust... ex. Carol Stinson "Trustee of 2015 1 Transaction Trust". There are some wholesalers that sign "Trustee, exact vesting TBD at closing." I do not see the need to put this in as long as you list the Trust as buyer on the Purchase Agreement and sign as Trustee. The property will close in the name of the Trust with you as Trustee. Therefore "vesting" does not need to be

determined at closing as it was already determined on the purchase agreement.

6. Once you have located an end buyer for your deal, you will be assigning your beneficial interest in the Land Trust to your buyer in exchange for you're agreed upon wholesale fee. Your end buyer will then bring the funds for the purchase of the property to closing, along with your fee.

7. List your buyer as Beneficiary on the Land Trust Agreement.

8. Bring the Trust Agreement that was endorsed by you and your buyer to closing.

Once the closing has taken place, your buyer (who is now the beneficiary of the Land Trust which owns the property), will fire you as the Trustee and appoint another.

You will have the Trust Agreement notarized at the closing table immediately following closing on the property and collect your fee. The Trust Agreement has already been signed by both you and your buyer. You are the Trustee and your buyer is the beneficiary (with full control of the Trust). You have already given the Trust Agreement to the closing Agent prior to closing and notarizing the Trust Agreement is the part where you get off. Once everything is notarized and you get paid the buyer can switch you out as Trustee and put in a replacement Trustee.

One thing to note is that a Land Trust is never created until closing because you must have a property to put into the Land Trust in order to create a Land Trust. Therefore the Trust is created simultaneously with the closing of the property. This is why you can wait until closing to put your Buyer into the beneficiary position of the Trust and collect your fee.

Also, with a land trust, the identity of the real owner is never disclosed to the public. Therefore once you declare the name of the "Buyer" on the purchase agreement as the Land Trust that you created there is no need to change it when your buyer steps into Beneficiary position. The property will close with the name of the Land Trust as buyer with your Buyer as beneficiary of that Land Trust. Therefore the deed never changes ownership when you add or change the beneficiaries and thus does not violate the deed restrictions set by the bank. This is the simplest, cut and dry way to transfer your interest in a property over to your buyer when wholesaling a Foreclosure or REO property.

So, to sum up, a trust is created by two documents: a "Trust document", which outlines the roles and responsibilities of the beneficiaries and trustee, and a "Deed", which conveys title to the newly created trust. The trust documents are not recorded so as to maintain privacy, but the deed is recorded in the name of the Land Trust. At closing the land trust agreement is given to your buyer along with the closing documents.

Since every state is different when it comes to the creation of a land trust make sure you check your local laws or consult an Attorney prior to adopting this method of wholesaling. Ask your Attorney to review the attached "Trust Agreement" and add or subtract items to make it uniform with your state's regulations. Once you get a master "Trust Agreement" in place that has been reviewed and edited by your Attorney you can simply keep using it to create Land Trusts. Once you have transferred the land trust to a buyer create another one and repeat the process.

Buying or wholesaling a property subject to the existing mortgage.

Land Trusts are not only a great tool for wholesaling properties but they are great for taking a property "Subject to the existing loan". A non-assumable loan can be assumed by using a land trust. This is a great strategy especially if the seller is facing imminent foreclosure because they can't pay their mortgage payments. By taking over the payments you are alleviating the seller from the damage to their credit from the foreclosure and you are preventing one more foreclosure from hitting a market that is already bogged down with too many foreclosures. It's also a win for the bank as the delinquent mortgage payments will be made current and will continue to be paid each month. Here's how it's done...

The seller transfers title into a land trust via a Quit Claim Deed, with you as beneficiary and the seller as Trustee. This transfer does not trigger the due-on-sale clause of the mortgage as the Seller still remains the Trustee of the Land Trust. The details of the Trust (names of Trustees, Beneficiaries etc...) is not recorded anywhere in public records. The only thing recorded is the Quit Claim Deed into the name of the Trust of which the seller is Trustee. This effectively makes a non-assumable loan "assumable".

Important to note * Get a PO Box in the name of the Land Trust and have ALL mail in regards to the property (Mortgage statements, water bill, sewer bill, tax bill etc...) forwarded to the PO Box. Once the new Quit Claim Deed is recorded in the County Records you can change the name on the utilities and tax records to the name of the Land Trust. In the end all of the bills and statements are in the name of the Land Trust being mailed to the PO Box created for the Land Trust.

As you can see there are many creative and effective uses for the Land Trust, limited only by your imagination!

Wholesaling another wholesaler's deal

There are so many ways to make money in wholesaling but some things require more creativity than others. Wholesaling is all about contracts. If you have the right contracts in place at the right time you can wholesale any property from any seller to any buyer…. it's that simple.

Wholesalers are " **Contract Geniuses**"! A great wholesaler should be able to come up with and edit any contract to meet the needs of a particular deal.

Let's face it we specialize in creating contracts that get our deals closed and get us paid. If we are honest with ourselves this is really what we are good at…. putting the right contracts in the right places to get paid.

Wholesalers all know how to wholesale a property from a seller to a buyer and get paid in the middle. You can either Assign the contract or double close the deal if it's an REO or short sale. But what about wholesaling another wholesaler's wholesale deal? What if you had a buyer for a deal that you knew another wholesaler had under contract? You're not going to connect the two for free or at least I hope not. Wholesaling another wholesaler's deal is something that I call "whotailing" as you are tailing behind another wholesaler's wholesale deal. To do this you must make sure you have the proper contracts in place to protect yourself and ensure that you get paid.

If you are simply assigning another deal over to your buyer that another wholesaler has under contract with a seller you will need an "Option Agreement" with the other Wholesaler giving you equitable interest in the property by giving you the option to purchase the property. Once you have the Option Contract in place with the other wholesaler you will need an Assignment Contract in place with your buyer.

This means there will be three contracts in place on a particular property:

1. Purchase Agreement between other wholesaler and seller.

2. Option Agreement between you and the other wholesaler. This contract will include the price that the other wholesaler is paying for the property plus the wholesaler's fee.

3. Assignment Contract between you and your buyer. This contract will include the price that you are paying the other wholesaler for the property (their purchase price plus their fee) and your fee, how much you will be making on the deal.

You will submit all of these contracts to the Title Company or closing Attorney.

What if the property is an REO and needs to double close?

You will need three contracts in place here as well.

1. Purchase Agreement between seller and other wholesaler.

   - This transaction would close first.

2. Purchase Agreement between you and the other wholesaler.

3. Assignment Contract between you and your buyer.

   - Now this deal closes and you get paid... aka, double close. You cannot assign the first transaction since it is an REO or Short Sale but you can assign the second transaction since the bank is no longer in the deal.

You must make sure that you have a contract in place with the other wholesaler before you introduce the property to your buyer. It is illegal to market a property that you do not have an equitable interest in. Your contract between you and the wholesaler gives you that equitable interest in the property. Also, the contract secures your position in the deal so you get paid. Never assume another wholesaler is going to pay you in the transaction without a contract. Always secure your position to secure your fee.

Chapter 6

CONTRACT BASICS

Your contract is the tie that binds you to the seller and the buyer. The contracts that you use in every transaction are basic real estate contracts. However you will need to change them a bit to make them work for you. You are assigning your interest in the contract not selling the house. Remember Realtors sell houses, wholesalers assign their equitable interest in the contract to a buyer. There is a big difference between selling and assigning and your contracts must protect your interest in the property and provide you with a way to get paid in the transaction.

Assigning a contract to a buyer

The best way to transfer a property over to a buyer is to assign your interest in that property via an Assignment Contract. An assignment is defined as:

" A transfer of rights in real property or Personal property to another that gives the recipient the rights that the owner or holder of the property had prior to the transfer."

The real estate assignment process involves 2 contracts, a Purchase Agreement and an Assignment Contract.

The Purchase Agreement

One method of wholesaling is by assigning your equitable interest in a property over to a buyer for a fee. This method is called an "assignment of contract". I know I stated this is Chapter 2, but I just want to reintegrate it again… "Because contract rights are considered property, they can be transferred to others just like a piece of property such as a home or car."

An "assignment of contract" is a process of transferring your rights, equitable interest, over to another buyer for a fee.

Make sure you put an option to assign on your contract. Options can be sold or exercised you can do this by putting "and/ or assign" next to your signature when you sign a purchase agreement with a seller this will enable you to assign the contract to another buyer.

There are two contracts that you will use in an assignment transaction. A Purchase Agreement and an Assignment Contract. The Purchase Agreement is the contract between you and the seller and the Assignment Contract is the contract between you and the buyer.

The Purchase Agreement or "Agreement of Sale" is a legally binding contract between you and the seller. Once you and the seller agree on a price you will fill out the purchase agreement with the information on the property and the agreed purchase price. Once both, the wholesaler and the seller, sign this contract you and the seller have a legally binding agreement. This is referred to as a property being "Locked Up". You have sealed the agreement between you and the seller with both of your signatures and therefore locked it up so no one else can buy the property. Now you have the right to market that property and find a buyer with the intention of assigning it over to that buyer for a fee.

The Assignment Contract

The Assignment Contract is the contract between you and the buyer. It is the contract that you will need in order to get paid in the transaction. The Assignment Contract is simply a contract between you and the buyer stating that you are assigning your rights and interests in the property over to the buyer for a fee. The fee is listed on the contract and will be distributed to you at the closing of the property.

Once the buyer signs the Assignment Contract he is agreeing to buy the property for your set price and pay you your fee to take over the contract.

Once you have both the Purchase Agreement and Assignment Contract signed you will take them both to your Title Company or Attorney for them to proceed with the closing of the deal.

Not all Title Companies and Attorneys will do assignments. You will want to check with your local Investors Club or other wholesalers in your area as they are already doing this in your area they will know of a Title Company or Attorney that does assignments.

Double closing on a property

There will be times when you cannot assign a property to a buyer because the purchase agreement between you and the seller has a non- assignment clause in it. This is common when a property is listed on the MLS. When there is a real estate agent between you and the seller you will be required to sign the purchase contract that the agent provides as this is their state mandated contract. This contract will have a non- assignment clause that prevents you from assigning the contract over to another buyer.

You will then need to double close on that property to get paid. The process of a double close involves 2 contracts. A Purchase Agreement between you and the seller and another separate Purchase Agreement between you and the buyer. Basically you will be using 2 Purchase Contracts instead of a Purchase Contract and an Assignment Contract.

Purchase Contract 1

This contract is the contract between you and the seller. You must close on your purchase from the seller first before you can sell the property to your buyer. This transaction is known as the A-B transaction. For this transaction you will need "Transactional Funding" or one day funding. Transactional funding is available for a fee from many money lenders. There are many sources available on the internet for this type of funding... One of the transactional funding sources that I have found useful is Besttransactionfunding.com.

You will need to close and fund the first transaction first and then close the second transaction immediately following the first closing.

Purchase Contract 2

This is the Purchase Agreement between you and your buyer. This transaction is known as the B-C transaction and closes immediately following the closing of the first transaction. For this transaction you can use your own Purchase Agreement. I have included a Purchase Agreement that you can download and print in MY WHOLESALING VAULT.

Exit clauses

An exit clause is a provision in a contract which allows for termination of the contract. Also called termination provision or a Shotgun Clause.

There are a few exit clauses that you will need to put on a standard purchase agreement to protect you in case you cannot find a buyer. These contingencies will give you a way out of the contract if you are unsuccessful in finding a buyer to take over your contract position.

The following exit clauses can be added to your purchase agreement when dealing with a FSBO property (one not listed with a Real Estate Agent).

When I prepare a FSBO purchase agreement I simply add the exit clauses below:

ASSIGNMENT: During the contract period before closing, buyer has the right to show potential buyers the property, place a for sale sign and lock box on the property, advertise the property, and market and/or list the on the multiple listing service (MLS) to sell property with the intention of freely assigning this contract and reselling this property. Buyer and Seller agree that Buyer intends to resell this property. If Buyer does not find a third party buyer for the property, buyer has the right to cancel this contract.

PARTNER APPROVAL: This contract is contingent upon Partner Approval.

The above exit clause simply states that if your partner does not approve the property purchase then the contract is void. Your partner is your buyer, therefore if you cannot find a buyer to approve the Purchase Agreement and buy the property then you can exit the contract.

14 DAY INSPECTION: This contract is contingent upon a satisfactory 14 day inspection period.

The above exit clause is put into the contract to give you time to find a buyer before the contract becomes binding between you and the seller. If after 13 days you cannot find a buyer to take over your contract you can exit the contract. On day 13 you would inform the seller that the property did not pass your inspection.

These are the three exit clauses that I incorporate into my Purchase Agreement on a FSBO property. When dealing with an Agent you must use their state approved Real Estate Purchase Agreement. The only exit clause that you can utilize on this contract is the 14 day inspection period. The Agent will write this exit clause into the contract for you. This exit clause is sufficient enough to allow you to exit the contract should you not find a buyer.

Chapter 7

WHOLESALING RESOURCES

Real estate wholesaling or doing efficient due diligence on a potential investment property would not be possible without the multitude of resources available to help with the process. Let's face it online resources, apps and other resources are a valuable tool to the Real Estate Investor and Wholesaler. With all of these resources at our fingertips there are no limits to our success!

BUT HOW DO YOU KNOW WHICH RESOURCES TO USE OR WHERE TO FIND THE RESOURCES THAT YOU NEED?

I have literally tried and tested hundreds of resources from websites to apps through the years and have tossed many of them. There are also some resources that I just cannot be without as they perform the very task that I need them to perform to make me successful. Some of these resources are free to use and some cost me a small monthly fee or are inexpensive to purchase, but trust me the resource pays for itself and then some.

I would like to share my TOP TEN REAL ESTATE WHOLESALING RESOURCES with you. These are my top ten real estate resources that I use on a daily basis and simply cannot live without. They are resources that I recommend you to try for yourself as I am confident you will find them to be an asset to your real estate investing or wholesaling business.

TEN OF MY FAVORITE WHOLESALING RESOURCES

1. AWebber

This is my #1 real estate wholesaling resource. This resource has enabled me to build my buyer's list to over 7,000 and counting.

2. HOMESNAP Real Estate & MLS Homes for Sale – Sawbuck

One of my favorite FREE real estate Apps! With this APP you can simply open the APP and take a picture of a property with your phone and HOME SNAP will immediately give you all of the information on that property. Listing price if it's for sale, similar properties for sale in the area and even the basic details of the subject property like sq. ft., beds baths etc… TRULY AWESOME APP!

3. RSMeans Contractor's Pricing Guide: Residential Repair & Remodeling 2014

This is the very price guide that my rehab company and many other contractors use to calculate rehab costs for a property. With this book a real estate wholesaler or Investor can quickly calculate the cost of materials, labor and demo of ANY rehab project. No need to have a Contractor go with you to estimate a rehab when you can do it yourself

4. Postlets.com

This FREE real estate resource allows you to create a property presentation flyer to market your wholesale property for sale. Postlets also has one-click syndication to 20+ sites. Plus, easy posting to Craigslist.

5. Zabasearch.com

Zabasearch is a FREE People Search and Public Information Search Engine. When I need to find the owner of a vacant property I jump on Zabasearch.com. I type in the property owners name that I get from the County real estate tax records and with a bit of digging I not only get their current address but sometimes I get really lucky and get their current phone number too!

5. **Zillow.com**

6. This FREE real estate resource enables you to evaluate a property and estimate the retail value of a property. In spite of all of the controversy about using Zillow for comps on a property I still find it the most accurate resource for property evaluation.

7. Rentometer.com

This FREE real estate resource enables you to determine the current rental amount for a property. Rentometer is the easy way to compare your rent with other local properties.

8. Legalzoom.com

With Legalzoom you can create an LLC for as little as $149. This is a great deal for Wholesalers who create numerous LLCs to flip REOs and Short sales.

9. WIX.com

Wix gives you everything you need to create a stunning FREE website, right at your fingertips. This is an awesome resource especially for those real estate wholesalers that are wholesaling in multiple states and need a place to send buyers and sellers in each state.

10. Google Voice

This FREE Google service provides a U.S. phone number, chosen by the user from available numbers in selected area codes, free of charge to each user account. This is a great resource for real estate wholesalers as you can chose a phone number with area code for whatever market you're currently wholesaling in. Many other Google Voice services—such as voicemail, free text messaging, call history, conference, call screening, blocking of unwanted calls, and voice transcription to text of voicemail messages—are also available to users.

Chapter 8

Mindset Matters

I have dedicated this book to providing you with everything that you will ever need to be successful at real estate wholesaling, therefore I could not end this book without stressing how much your mindset plays a huge part in your success. You can learn all of the strategies, gain all of the resources and knowledge, but if your mind is not in the game you will never succeed.

Don't chase the money, chase the vision!

When I first started in real estate I learned the hard way that chasing the money without a vision always ended up with me chasing money! The whole idea is that when you chase money you get just that, YOU CHASING MONEY! You might be able to catch it once in a while and make a few bucks here and there but it's like holding onto a greased pig. You can only hold on for a very short time unless you have the right mindset, the mindset of success.

If you create a vision, begin to believe in yourself and develop a mindset that backs that vision then, and only then, will you have the right vision and mindset to begin making the money. I made my first $10,000.00 within 30 days of starting in real estate and then I got comfortable. But, when things got rough again, I began wanting to quickly make more money in an effort to simply survive. I had a survival mindset instead of a thriving mindset and as a result I was chasing the money without creating a vision. People who want to simply survive will chase the money, people who want to thrive will chase their vision.

I suggest that you focus on the change that you want to see in your life, the dream that you have. WHY do you want to do this? WHY do you want to be successful? Once you know your WHY then create your vision. Once you create your vision, develop your mindset to back your vision and then you will see the money start to come to you. By chasing your vision and implementing the steps needed to make the money, the money will start coming to you instead of you chasing the money.

By chasing the change, the vision, you will be setting yourself up for success. The foundation will be confident, wise and unstoppable! Once you have built the foundation the money will come!

There is a story in the Bible about a wise man and a foolish man. The wise man built his house upon a rock and the winds blew, the floods came and beat upon that house and it did not fall. However a foolish man built his house upon the sand and the winds blew and the floods came and beat upon that house and it came falling down with a crash!

By focusing on the change and building self-confidence you are building your house upon a rock and when the storms blow, and they will, you will withstand it and keep chasing your dream. If you focus on the change you need to make to achieve your dream you will stay strong when things don't go right. However, if you chase the money without the vision you will be setting yourself up for disappointment and failure when the money don't come as fast as you need it to. With the right mindset that backs your vision you will have strategies in place and know what you need to do to ensure the money will continuously come to you.

You can simply keep chasing the money, many do, but they are usually the ones who blow it once they get it and are immediately back chasing the money again. Money chasing without a vision and mindset change is a viscous cycle. One that will keep you broke and chasing money for the rest of your life. These are the people who have built their house upon the sand and when the storm blows they give up and say it don't work and find something else that will make them a quick buck. Money chasing will burn you out real quick!

Chase the vision, develop your mindset to back your vision and the money will come.

You must create a personal vision that encompasses what you want to **have** in your life, what you want to **do**, and the person you want to **be**. If you don't develop your own vision, you will be allowing other people and circumstances to then direct the course of your life. By creating your vision by writing it down you are more likely to succeed far beyond what you could otherwise achieve without a clear vision. Think of creating a vision like drawing a map from where you are now to where you want to be.

If you don't make an effort to visualize who you are and what you want in life, then you give that power over to other people and circumstances to create your life by default. You must have a clear vision of what you want for your life and then develop the action steps needed to obtain it. Vision first, action second.

People, places and things

I cannot stress enough how important it is to surround yourself with the people who are already successful at real estate. People who are already doing it! They know that it can be done, that money can be made in real estate because they are doing it. By surrounding yourself with these people you will stay encouraged and therefore be successful.

To spend time with these people you must go where they are. The Real Estate Investor meetings. You can find out where there is a meeting near you by visiting **meetup.com.** This website will give you information, address and times they meet. I suggest that you go to as many as you can when you can. This is a great way to meet others that share a similar mindset for real estate.

You must also do the things that they do. Ask other wholesalers and buyers at the meeting what is working for them in your local real estate market. How are they finding deals? What marketing strategies are working best for them?

They have been in your market longer than you so pick their brain so you can reproduce their success.

If you want to be successful you must be around successful people, learn from them and socialize with them. Go where they are and do what they do.

FROM THE AUTHOR

I was born and raised in the city of brotherly love (Philadelphia) and I currently reside in Southern NJ. I make a good living investing in real estate and wholesaling real estate around the Country.

I am not a real estate Guru, I don't live a super fancy life yet I am the most blessed person in the world! I have a wonderful husband, 5 beautiful children and 3 grandchildren and I make a great income, who could ask for more?

Like most people who grew up in Philadelphia, I grew up in poverty. I got married when I was 19 years old and my husband and I always lived pay check to pay check. The problem with this way of living is that when the paycheck stops coming you stop living. I had always wanted more out of life but never knew how to change my current circumstances. I didn't have a college education, lacked special job skills and honestly did not have an entrepreneurial mindset. I was always a stay at home mom and my husband ran our family rehab business. This business kept us financially afloat for many years however when the economy took a tumble in 2008 our business took a tumble as well. This was the year that I was introduced to real estate wholesaling.

I was introduced to real estate wholesaling in 2008 and made $10,000.00 in my first 30 days. Today I buy and rehab properties in NJ and wholesale real estate across the Country.

WHY DID I WRITE EVERYTHING WHOLESALING?

I am currently earning 6 figures a year wholesaling real estate from home. I am living my dream life and earning more money than I ever thought possible. I am on my way to total financial freedom and my desire is to take as many people with me as possible. There are many still living with the mindset of thinking

"This is it" but let me tell you there is so much more out there for you.

I wrote the EVERYTHING WHOLESALING GUIDE to share my knowledge and experience with others in the hope that I can help someone else achieve the financial freedom that I have achieved through real estate.

By sharing the strategies that work in today's real estate market and helping others get started in real estate I am paying it forward. If you are ready to live the life you have always dreamed of, ready to change your life and obtain financial freedom I am here to help you every step of the way.

And finally, please read this carefully:

I don't consider myself a real estate guru, my techniques are not secrets and what I teach are not "get rich quick" schemes – far from it actually.

I know I have an inspiring story and I am here to inspire you too, however I want to do it the right way. I speak only from my experience and please don't feel like you owe me anything because of it. This is my way of paying it forward and leading you through the amazing journey to financial freedom that I have had the privilege of experiencing.

You won't get any hard sells from me, long sales pages or fluffed up stuff – just real life strategies that I have tried and proved and recommendations based on my own experiences.

My hope is that through my experience and proven strategies you too will gain finical freedom through real estate. I have given you everything that you need to make it happen… the rest is up to you.

To Your Success,

Carol Stinson

MY WHOLEALING VAULT

Now is the time to go access

MY WHOLESALING VAULT

Go to mywholesalingvault.com where you will be able to edit and print the following contracts as needed. Plus… step by step videos on how to fill out each contract and more.

CONTRACTS

CONTRACT FOR SALE OF REAL ESTATE

CONTRACT FOR SALE OF REAL ESTATE

This CONTRACT is made and dated _____ between
_____, whose address is
_____ (referred to as the "Seller"), AND
_____, whose address is
_____ (referred to as "Buyer") and/or
assigns. The words "Seller" and "Buyer" include all sellers and all buyers
under this Contract.

1. <u>SALE AND PURCHASE</u>: The Seller agrees to sell and the Buyer
   agrees to buy the Property described in this Contract.
2. <u>PROPERTY</u>: The word "Property" in this Contract includes the
   building, land, improvements thereon and fixtures on the land
   situated in the Township of _____ , County of
   _____, and State of _____, commonly known
   as _____ and is shown on the
   municipal tax map as
   Lot_____ Block_____, which is owned by the
   Seller.

3. <u>PERSONAL PROPERTY AND FIXTURES</u>: The property being
   transferred includes

   _____

4. <u>PURCHASE PRICE AND MANNER OF PAYMENT</u>: The
   purchase price is _____ Dollars. The
   Buyer will pay the purchase price as follows:

   Cash at closing _____

   Total Purchase Price (Paid at closing)   _____

4. <u>CLOSING TIME AND PLACE</u>: Closing is the meeting at which the
Seller transfers ownership of the property by Deed to the Buyer and the
Buyer pays the Seller the remainder of the purchase price. Closing
shall take place on or before _____at (Name of Title Agency)
_____ The Seller shall have the privilege of

paying off any persons with a claim or right affecting the property from the proceeds of the sale at the time of settlement.

5. TITLE:

(a)   The title to the Property shall be transferred in fee simple by bargain and sale deed with covenants against grantor's acts. The deed shall be in proper form for recording. The Seller shall also give the Buyer a sworn statement known as an affidavit of title. The affidavit shall contain information about the Seller reasonably necessary to clarify the Seller's ownership of the property. Title shall be good and marketable, and except as otherwise provided in the Contract, shall be free and clear of all encumbrances, including municipal liens and assessments and liability for assessments for improvements now constructed. Title is to be subject to all existing agreements, restrictions and easements of record. The Seller states there are no restrictions which will prohibit the use and/or occupancy of the property as a single family dwelling unit. A violation of any restriction shall not be a reason for Buyer refusing to complete settlement as long as the title company insures the Buyer against actual loss at regular rates.

(b)   In the event the Seller is unable to transfer the quality of title required and if the Buyer is unwilling to accept Seller's title, this Contract shall terminate, the Deposit shall be returned to Buyer, and neither party shall have any further claim against the other.

6. PROPERTY SURVEY: The Buyer has the right to survey the property using a licensed surveyor. The cost associated with this service shall be the responsibility of the Buyer.

7. CONDITION OF PROPERTY`: The Property (land and building) shall be transferred in the same condition as it now appears. This means that the Property is being sold "AS IS". Contract is contingent upon a 14 day inspection period.

8. UNDERGROUND FUEL TANKS: Seller states, to the best of Seller's knowledge, there is/are no underground fuel tanks nor have there been any removed. **This contract is contingent upon inspection and testing of the underground oil tank.**

9. SELLER NOT LIABLE TO BUYER AFTER SETTLEMENT

All warranties, guarantees, representations of Seller concerning the property, the systems servicing the property, the appliances, lot lines, location of structures, driveways, fences and any other matter affecting this Contract, unless otherwise set forth in writing shall be absolutely void after settlement or delivery and acceptance of possession or occupancy, whichever is earlier

10. POSSESSION: Buyer shall be given ownership of the Property at Closing free and clear of any third party's claim to possession. Title to the Property will transfer to Buyer at the time of Closing.

11. CLOSING COSTS AND ADJUSTMENTS: Seller shall pay for the closing costs including the preparation of the Deed, realty transfer tax, and one-half of the attendance allowed by the Commissioner of Insurance. Buyer shall be responsible for searches, title insurance, and one half of the attendance allowed by the Commissioner of Insurance. Seller shall be responsible for any other liens, unpaid taxes, and judgments required to convey clear title. The Seller and the Buyer agree that there shall be an apportionment of the following costs at settlement have been paid by Seller or are due from Seller such as: (a) municipal real estate taxes, and (b) water and sewer charges if any.

12. NOTICES: All notices required in this Contract must be in writing. All notices shall be by certified mail, by facsimile transmission, or by personal delivery. The certified letter or facsimile transmission will be effective upon sending. The personal delivery will be effective upon delivery to the other party. Each party must accept the certified mail or facsimile transmission sent by the other party. Notices sent must be properly addressed and directed to the party to receive the same at the address written at the beginning of this Contract. Either party may designate a different person or entity or place to or at which notices shall be given by delivering a written notice to that effect to the other party, which notice shall be effective after the same is actually received by the other party.

13. RISK OF LOSS: The risk of loss or damage to the property by fire or otherwise, accepting ordinary wear and tear is the liability of the Seller until closing.

14. SELLER'S DEFAULT: In the event the Seller fails to make settlement in accordance with this Contract, the Buyer may commence any legal or equitable action to which the Buyer may be entitled.

15. BUYER'S DEFAULT: In the event the Buyer fails to make settlement in accordance with this Contract, the Seller may commence any legal or equitable action to which the Seller is entitled.

16. <u>ZONING</u>: The Seller makes no representation concerning existing zoning ordinances except that the Seller's use of the single family dwelling unit may be continued.

17. <u>FLOOD AREAS</u>: The federal and state governments have designated certain areas as flood areas. If the property is located in a flood area, the use of the property may be limited. The Seller is not aware that the property is in a "flood area". However, if Buyer's inquiry reveals that the property is in a "flood area", the Buyer shall obtain flood insurance.

18. This contract is contingent upon partnership approval.

19. <u>NO RELIANCE ON OTHERS</u>: This Contract is entered into by the Seller and Buyer based upon their independent knowledge of the value of the property and their full understanding of the meaning of all the provisions of this Contract and not on any representations made by either of them to the other.

20. <u>ENTIRE AGREEMENT</u>: This Contract is the entire agreement of the Buyer and Seller. Neither party has made any other agreement or promise that is not included in this Contract. This Contract may be changed only if in writing and signed by both parties. Any representation not contained in this Contract are of no effect.

21. <u>CHANGES IN CONTRACT</u>: The parties may not change this contract unless the change is in writing and signed by both parties.

22. <u>ASSIGNMENT</u>: During the contract period before closing, buyer has the right to show potential Investors/ partners the property and assign this contract.

23. <u>CONSTRUCTION</u>: This Contract was made and executed in the State of New Jersey and shall be governed by and construed according to the laws of the State of New Jersey.

24. <u>BINDING ON SUCCESSORS</u>: This Contract is binding not only on the Seller and the Buyer, but also on their heirs, personal representatives, successors and lawful assigns.

25. <u>ATTORNEY REVIEW</u>: The Buyer or Seller may choose to have an attorney study this Contract. If an attorney is consulted, the attorney must complete his or her Review of the Contracts within a three-day period. This Contract will be legally binding at the end of this three-day period unless an

attorney for the Buyer or the Seller reviews and disapproves of this Contract. You count the three days from the date of delivery of the signed Contract to Buyer and Seller. You do not count Saturdays, Sundays, or legal holidays. The Buyer and the Seller may agree in writing to extend the three-day period for Attorney review. In the event that an attorney for the Buyer or the Seller disapproves of the Contract, the attorney must send notice of disapproval to the Buyer or the Seller by certified mail, by facsimile, or by delivering it personally. The facsimile or certified letter will be effective upon sending. The personal delivery will be effective upon delivery. In the event of cancellation, this Contract shall terminate, the Deposit shall be returned to Buyer, and neither party shall have any further claim against the other.

The Seller and the Buyer agree to the terms of this Contract by signing below.

SELLER:

Sign: _____

(Print name here)

Sign: _____

(Print name here)

Date Signed _____

WITNESS:

Sign: _____

BUYER:

Sign: _____

(Print name here)

_____

Sign:

_____

(Print name here)

Date Signed _____

ASSIGNMENT OF CONTRACT

ASSIGNMENT OF CONTRACT

The undersigned _____ (Assignor), having executed a contract dated _____ between _____ (Seller), assigns all right, title and interest in said agreement to _____ (Assignee) concerning the property described as _____ in exchange for compensation in the amount of _____.

Assignee agrees to fulfill all terms, conditions and contingencies of said contract and to perform as required in good faith and within any time periods established by said contract.

1. The buyer will close on the property by _____.

2. The owner will pay all taxes and fees due up to the date of closing.

3. The property is understood to be sold "as is".

4. Said property is to be sold free and clear of all encumbrances, by good and marketable title, with full possession to said property available to buyer at the date of closing.

Assignee further agrees to hold assignors harmless from any deficiencies and defects in the legality or the enforceability of the terms of said agreement. The parties hereby agree, understand and acknowledge that the Assignor is an Investor and is not acting as an Agent, employee, Broker, representative or fiduciary for SELLER or ASSIGNEE, but acting solely in the INVESTOR'S own behalf as principal of transaction, and that all profits made herein are not a commission, fee, finder's fee, or employment compensation.

Assignment to be paid out as follows:

- Name _____
- Amount _____

_____ Date: _____
Assignor

_____ Date: _____
Assignee

SALE OF LLC INTEREST AGREEMENT

SALE OF LLC INTEREST AGREEMENT

This Agreement is entered this the _____ day of _____, 20___, by and between _____, hereinafter referred to as Seller, and _____ (Name), hereinafter referred to as Purchaser.

WITNESSETH:

WHEREAS, the parties hereto desire that _____ percent (_____%) interest in the capital and profits of _____., hereinafter referred to as LLC, be sold to Purchaser pursuant to this Agreement on the date and at the time provided for herein _____(the "Effective Date"); and

WHEREAS, the parties hereto desire to set forth certain representations, warranties, and covenants made by each to the other as an inducement to the consummation of the sale and certain additional agreements related to the sale;

NOW, THEREFORE, in consideration of the premises and of the mutual representations, warranties, and covenants herein contained, the parties hereby agree as follows:

ARTICLE I

1.1 Subject to the terms and conditions set forth herein, the closing of this sale of LLC interest shall be held on

_____.

1.2 The Seller shall sell the said LLC interest for a total purchase price of _____ ($_____).

1.3 The Seller shall tender to Purchaser at the closing a fully executed bill of sale for the interest being transferred.

1.4 The Purchaser shall deliver a non-refundable deposit in the amount of _____ ($_____) at the time of executing this agreement. The balance shall delivered at the closing by certified or cashier's check in the amount of

_____

($_____).

ARTICLE II

2.1 Seller represents and warrants to Purchaser that as of the date hereof and on the Effective Date (all representations and warranties being joint and several):

(a) To the best of Sellers knowledge and belief, the LLC has good and marketable title to all properties, assets, and leasehold estates, real and personal, as set forth in the attached Exhibit A, subject to no mortgage, pledge, lien, conditional sales agreement, encumbrance, or charge.

(b) The Seller has delivered to Purchaser a list (Schedule 1), complete in all material respects, as of _____, of all insurance policies carried by the LLC. The LLC carries insurance on its properties, assets, and business, which Seller believes to be adequate in character and amount, with reputable insurers and such insurance policies are still in full force and effect.

(c) In all respects material to the business, financial condition, and properties of the LLC on a consolidated basis, the LLC is not in default under any law or regulation, or under any order of any court or federal, state, municipal, or other governmental department, commission, board, bureau, agency, or instrumentality wherever located, and, except to the extent set forth on the attached Schedule 2 there are (1) no claims, actions, suits, or proceedings instituted or filed or, (2) to the knowledge of the Seller there are no claims, actions, suits, or proceedings threatened presently or which in the future may be threatened against or affecting the LLC at law or in equity, or before or by any federal, state, municipal, or other governmental department, commission, board, bureau, agency, or instrumentality wherever located.

ARTICLE III

3.1 At or before the Closing Date:

(a) The Seller's Members (or Seller and the other Members of the LLC if Seller is not the LLC itself) will cause Seller (or LLC if Seller is not the LLC itself) to:

(1) Carry on its business substantially as it has heretofore and not introduce any materially new method of management, operation or accounting;

(2) perform all material obligations under agreements which relate to or affect its assets, properties, and rights;

(3) Use its best efforts to maintain and preserve its business organization intact, retain its present employees, and maintain its relationships with suppliers, customers, and others having business relations with them;

(4) Maintain its properties and facilities in as good working order and condition as at present, ordinary wear and tear excepted; and

(5) Keep in full force and effect present insurance policies or other comparable insurance coverage.

(b) The Members will not permit the Seller (or if the LLC itself is not the Seller: The Seller and the other Members of the LLC will not permit the LLC), without the prior written consent of the Purchaser, to:

(1) Enter into any contract or commitment or incur or agree to incur any liability or make any capital expenditures except in the normal course of business;

(2) Create, assume, or permit to exist any mortgage, pledge, or other lien or encumbrance upon any assets or properties whether now owned or hereafter acquired;

(3) Increase the compensation payable or to become payable to any Member, employee, or agent, or make any bonus payment to any such person; or

(4) Sell, assign, lease, or otherwise transfer or dispose of any property or equipment except in the normal course of business.

ARTICLE IV

4.1 The Sellers obligations hereunder are, at its option, subject to the satisfaction of the following condition on or prior to the Effective Date:

(a) If Purchaser is a corporation, the Seller shall have received a copy of the resolutions authorizing the execution, delivery, and performance of this Agreement by Purchaser certified by the Secretary of Purchaser to have been adopted by Purchasers Board of Directors and to be in full force and effect as of the Effective Date.

ARTICLE V

5.1 If Purchaser is a corporation, Purchaser represents and warrants to Seller as of the date hereof and on the Effective Date, that the execution, delivery, and performance of this Agreement by Purchaser has been duly authorized by Purchasers Board of Directors and that the Agreement constitutes the valid and binding obligation of Purchaser and that a properly certified Board of Directors resolution to this effect will be presented to Seller before the Effective Date.

ARTICLE VI

6.1 The parties hereto shall deliver or cause to be delivered on the Effective Date, and at such other times and places as shall be reasonably agreed on, such additional instruments as may reasonably be requested for the purpose of carrying out this Agreement. Seller will cooperate and use its best efforts to have the present Members and employees of Seller (or LLC if the LLC itself is not the Seller) cooperate on and after the Effective Date in furnishing information, evidence, testimony, and other assistance in connection with any actions, proceedings, arrangements, or disputes of any nature with respect to matters pertaining to all periods prior to the Effective Date.

6.2 This Agreement (including the schedules and annexes hereto) and the documents delivered pursuant hereto constitute the entire agreement and understanding between the parties and supersede any prior agreement and/or understanding relating to the subject matter of this Agreement. This Agreement may only be modified or amended by a duly authorized written instrument executed by the parties hereto.

6.3 This Agreement may be executed simultaneously in two or more counterparts. Each counterpart shall be deemed an original, and all of the counterparts together shall constitute but one and the same instrument.

6.4 Any notice or communication required or permitted hereunder shall be sufficiently given if sent by certified or registered mail, postage prepaid, with return receipt requested:

(a) To Purchaser at:

_____

_____

_____

(b) To Seller at:

_____

_____

_____

6.5 All warranties, covenants, representations, and guarantees shall survive the closing and execution of the documents contemplated by this Agreement. In executing and carrying out the provisions of this Agreement, the parties hereto are relying solely on the representations, warranties, and agreements contained in this Agreement or in any writing delivered pursuant to its provisions or at the closing of the transactions herein provided for and not upon any representation, warranty, agreement, promise, or information, written or oral, made by any person other than as specifically set forth herein or therein.

6.6 This Agreement shall be construed in accordance with the laws of the State of _____.

IN WITNESS WHEREOF, the parties have executed this Agreement as of the day and year first above written.

_____
Purchaser

_____
Seller

Witnesses:

_____

_____

_____

STATE OF _____

County of _____

On this _____ day of _____, ___, before me personally appeared _____, known to me to be the person described in and who executed the foregoing instrument and

acknowledged that he or she executed the same as
_____s own free act and deed.

_____
Notary Public
_____ (County)

_____ (State)
My Commission Expires: _____

TRUST AGREEMENT

TRUST AGREEMENT

Trust Agreement made this _____ day of _____, 20_____.

_____, Grantor(s)/
Settlor(s) and Beneficiaries, (hereinafter collectively referred to as the
"Beneficiaries"), whose address is,

_____

and_____, as Trustee of the trust
created hereby, (hereinafter referred to as the "Trustee", which designation
shall include all successor trustees), whose address is

∴

Whereas, the Beneficiaries are about to convey or cause to be
conveyed in the near future certain real property to the Trustee, and the
Trustee has agreed to accept such conveyance and hold the real property as
a fiduciary in trust for the Beneficiaries under the terms and conditions set
forth below.

Now, therefore, the parties hereby agree as follows:

1. Declaration of Trust. The trust created by the settlors herein
shall be known as the

_____

(hereinafter referred to as the "Trust").

2. Trust Property. The corpus of the trust will be real property
(hereinafter referred to as the "Trust Property") that the Beneficiaries will
convey or cause to be conveyed fee simple absolute by deed. Said property
is described in the attached Exhibit "A." The Trustee shall hold full legal
and equitable title to said property, in trust, only for the use and purpose
stated under the terms of this Agreement and any valid addendum hereto
duly executed by the parties. If permissible in the state in which the real
property sits, title shall be held in the name of the Trust itself, to wit: "
Trust," otherwise, the Trustee shall hold title in his or her name "an
individual, as Trustee, and not personally, of the _____
Trust"

3. <u>Trust Purpose</u>. The objects and purposes of this Trust shall be to hold full legal and equitable title to the Trust Property until its sale, disposition or liquidation, or until the trust is terminated or expires by its own terms and/or as a matter of law. The Trustee shall not undertake any activity that is not strictly necessary to the achievement of the foregoing objects and purposes, nor shall the Trustee transact business within the meaning of applicable state law, or any other law, nor shall this Agreement be deemed to be, or create or evidence the existence of a corporation, de facto or de jure, or a Massachusetts Trust, or any other type of business trust, or an association in the nature of a corporation, or a co-partnership or joint venture, limited liability company, or similar limited liability association by or between the Trustee and the Beneficiaries, or by or between the Beneficiaries.

4. <u>Consideration</u>. The Trustee has paid no consideration for the conveyance of real property described herein. The conveyance will be accepted and held by the Trustee subject to all existing liens, encumbrances, easements, restrictions or other clouds or claims against the title thereto, whether the same area of record or otherwise. The property will be held on the trusts, terms and conditions and for the purposes hereinafter set forth, until the whole of the trust estate is conveyed, free of this trust, as hereinafter provided.

5. <u>Rights and Duties of the Beneficiaries</u>. The persons and/or entities named in the attached Exhibit "B" (including their heirs, assigns or successors) hereof are the Beneficiaries of this Trust, and as such, shall be entitled to all of the earnings, avails and proceeds of the Trust Property according to their interests set opposite their respective names. No Beneficiary shall have any legal or equitable right, title or interest, as realty, in or to any real estate held in trust under this Agreement, or the right to require partition of that real estate, but shall have only the rights, as personally, set out below, and the death of a Beneficiary shall not terminate this Trust or in any manner affect the powers of the Trustee.

The interests of the Beneficiaries shall consist solely of the following rights respecting the Trust Property:

a. The right to direct the Trustee to convey or otherwise deal with the title to the Trust Property as hereinafter set out.

b. The right to participate in the management and control the Trust Property.

c. The right to receive the proceeds and avails from the rental, sale, mortgage, or other disposition of the Trust Property.

6. <u>Powers and Duties of Trustee</u>. The Trustee shall not copy or show this agreement to any individual or entity other than the beneficiaries or successor trustees, nor shall the Trustee reveal the identity of the beneficiaries or the trust property to any individual or entity except by way of a Court Order duly executed by a Justice or Magistrate of a Court of competent jurisdiction. The trustee shall not record this agreement or the name of any of the beneficiaries in any place of public record.

The Trustee, as the sole owner of record of the Trust Property, have the following powers with respect the Trust Property, at to the written direction of the Beneficiary:

a. To issue notes or bonds and to secure the payment of the same by executing a deed of trust, mortgage or other security instrument conveying a lien on the whole or any part of the Trust Property;

b. To borrow money, giving notes therefor, or to assume existing debts related to the property signed by him or her in the capacity as Trustee;

c. To invest such part of the capital and profits therefrom and the proceeds of the sale of bonds and notes in such real estate, equities in real estate, and mortgages in real estate in the United States of America;

d. To have, together with, and at the direction of the beneficiaries, the exclusive management and control of the property as if he were the absolute owner thereof, and the full power to do all things and perform all acts which in his or her judgment are necessary and proper for the protection and preservation of the Trust Property and for the interest of the Beneficiaries in the property of the Trust, subject to the restrictions, terms, and conditions set forth herein;

e. To take possession of the trust property in the event it becomes vacant;

f. To purchase any additional real property for the Trust at such times and on such terms as may be beneficial to the beneficiary;

g. To rent or lease the whole or any part of the Trust Property for long or short terms, but not for terms exceeding the term of the Trust then remaining;

h. To repair, alter, tear down, add to, or erect any building or buildings upon land belonging to the Trust; to fill, grade, drain, improve, and otherwise develop any land belonging to the Trust; to carry on, operate, or manage any building, apartment house, mobile home lot or hotel belonging to the Trust;

I. To make, execute, acknowledge, and deliver all deeds, releases, mortgages, leases, contracts, options, agreements, instruments, and other obligations of whatsoever nature relating to the Trust Property, and generally to have full power to do all things and perform all acts necessary to make the instruments proper and legal (and to do so by a duly appointed attorney-in-fact);

j. To collect notes, rents, obligations, dividends, and all other payments that may be due and payable to the Trust; to deposit the net proceeds thereof, as well as any other moneys from whatsoever source they may be derived, in any suitable bank or depository, and to draw the same from time to time for the purposes herein provided, paying the net proceeds therefrom to the beneficiaries;

k. To pay all lawful taxes and assessments and the necessary expenses of the Trust; to employ such officers, brokers, property managers, engineers, architects, carpenters, contractors, agents, counsel, and such other persons as may seem expedient, to designate their duties and fix their compensation; to fix a reasonable compensation for their own services to the Trust, as organizers thereof.

l. To represent the Trust and the Beneficiaries in all suits and legal proceedings relating to the Trust Property in any court of law of equity, or before any other bodies or tribunals; to begin suits and to prosecute them to final judgment or decree; to compromise claims or suits, and to submit the same to arbitration when, in their judgment, such course is necessary or proper.

Trustee in addition to the other duties herein imposed upon him or her, shall have the obligation to:

n. To keep a careful and complete record of all the beneficial interests in the Trust Property with the name and residence of the person or persons owning such beneficial interest, and such other items as they may deem of importance or as may be required by the Beneficiaries.

o. To keep careful and accurate books showing the receipts and disbursements he or she has made on behalf of the Trust and also of the Trust Property and to keep books of the Trust open to the inspection of the Beneficiaries.

Nothing in this agreement shall preclude the powers and authorities of a trustee as defined by state law, code or statute, unless such additional powers shall cause this agreement to be construed as a "trust" as defined in Section 301.7701-4(a) of the Procedure and Administration Regulations of the Internal Revenue Code.

7. Compensation of Trustee. The Beneficiaries jointly and severally agree that the Trustee shall receive the sum of $ per year for his or her services as Trustee.

8. Liability of Trustee. The Trustee and his or her successor as Trustee shall not be required to give a bond, and each Trustee shall be liable only for his own acts and then only as a result of his own gross negligence or bad faith.

9. Removal of Trustee. The Beneficiaries shall have the power to remove a Trustee from his office or appoint a successor to succeed him or her. This removal must by in writing, signed by all of the beneficiaries. Upon Seven (7) days written notice, the Trustee shall deliver all books, records, bank account information, keys, security deposits, leases and funds in his or her possession, and execute any documents necessary to convey title and/or authority over the Trust and the Trust Property to the Successor Trustee.

10. Resignation of Trustee. Any Trustee may resign his or her office with thirty (30) days written notice to Beneficiaries. The Beneficiaries shall appoint the Trustee named as successor Trustee herein

(or proceed to elect a new Trustee) to take the place of the Trustee who had resigned, but the resignation shall not take effect until an affidavit signed and acknowledged before a notary public by both the resigning Trustee and the new Trustee shall have been procured in a form which is acceptable for recording in the registries of deeds of all the counties in which properties held under this instrument are situated. If the Trust property is recorded in the name of the trustee himself, the resigning trustee shall also execute a general warranty deed in the proper form and manner for recording the registry of deeds in the county in which the property is situate. Said deed and/or affidavit need not be recorded unless so requested of the new Trustee at the written direction of the Beneficiaries.

In the event a new trustee is not appointed within Sixty (60) days after notice the resignation of the existing Trustee is received by the beneficiaries, this agreement shall terminate, and the resigning Trustee shall deliver all books, records, bank account information, keys, security deposits, leases and funds in his or her possession, and execute any documents necessary to convey title to the trust property to the beneficiaries as their interests may appear.

Whenever a new Trustee shall have been elected or appointed to the office of Trustee and shall have assumed the duties of office, he or she shall succeed to the title of all the properties of the Trust and shall have all the powers and be subject to all the restrictions granted to or imposed upon the Trustee by this agreement, and every Trustee shall have the same powers, rights, and interests regarding the Trust Property, and shall be subject to the same restrictions and duties as the original Trustee, except as the same shall have been modified by amendment, as herein provided for.

11. <u>Death or Incapacity of Trustee</u>. Upon the death, termination, resignation or physical or mental incapacity of the Trustee, the following individual(s) shall immediately be appointed as successor Trustee, with the full powers and duties of the former Trustee:

_____whose address is

_____,

Or, if said individual is not then living or is unable or unwilling to act as trustee, then_____, whose address is

_____,

In the event none of said individuals are then living or are unable or unwilling to act as Trustee, then a new Trustee will be elected and appointed as per paragraph "10" herein.

In the event of the death of any beneficiary, his or her right and interest hereunder, except as otherwise provided, shall pass to his or her executor or administrator and to his heirs at law.

12. <u>Beneficiary not Bound by Trustee</u>. The Trustee is not an agent or partner of, and shall have no power to bind the Beneficiaries personally and, in every written contract he may enter into, reference shall be made to this declaration; and any person or corporation contracting with the Trustee, as well as any beneficiary, shall look to the funds and the Trust Property for payment under such contract, or for the payment of any debt, mortgage, judgment, or decree, or for any money that may otherwise become due or payable, whether by reason or failure of the Trustee to perform the contract, or for any other reason, and neither the Trustee nor the Beneficiaries shall be liable personally therefor.

13. <u>Dealings with Trustee</u>. No party dealing with the Trustee in relation to the Trust Property in any manner whatsoever, and, without limiting the foregoing, no party to whom the property or any part of it or any interest in it shall be conveyed, contracted to be sold, leased or mortgaged by the Trustee, shall be obliged to see to the application of any purchase money, rent or money borrowed or otherwise advanced on the property; to see that the terms of this Trust Agreement have been complied with; to inquire into the authority, necessity or expediency of any act of the Trustee; or be privileged to inquire into any of the terms of this Trust Agreement.

14. <u>Recording of Agreement</u>. Neither this Agreement nor any summary of the contents hereof shall be placed on record in the county in which the Trust Property is situated, or elsewhere, but if it is so recorded, that recording shall not be considered as notice of the rights of any person under this Agreement derogatory to the title or powers of the Trustee.

15. <u>Term of Agreement</u>. This agreement shall continue for a period of twenty years from the date of its execution. The Trustee shall contact all Beneficiaries in writing at least twelve months prior to that time. The trustee shall place the Trust Property for public sale, pay all debts due

and owing with regard to the Trust Property, and remit the proceeds to the Beneficiaries according to their respective interests in the Trust. The Beneficiaries may choose to renew this agreement for a term of twenty additional years by submitting their intention in writing to the Trustee.

If any portion of the Trust Property is in any manner or time period capable of being held in this Land Trust for longer period of time than is permitted under the laws of the state law governing this Agreement, or the vesting of any interest under this Land Trust could possibly occur after the end of such permitted time period, then, upon the occurrence of the foregoing, the Trustee is directed to immediately terminate the Trust and to distribute the Trust Property to the Beneficiaries as their respective interests may appear at the time of the termination of the Trust. As much as possible, the Trustee will maintain the Trust Property intact and not liquidate it, but, rather, distribute the Trust Property in kind.

16. <u>Income Tax Returns</u>. The Trustee shall not be obligated to file any income tax returns with respect to the Trust, except as required by law, and the Beneficiaries individually shall report and pay their share of income taxes on the earnings and avails of the Trust Property or   growing out of their interest under this Trust. In the event an informational return is required by law, the Trustee agrees to execute the same after contacting all the Beneficiaries. It is the intention of the parties that this agreement does not create a "trust" under the definition as set forth in Section 301.7701-4(a) of the Procedure and Administration Regulations of the Internal Revenue Code.

17. <u>Assignment of Beneficial Interest</u>. The interest of a Beneficiary, or any part of that interest, may be transferred only by a written assignment, executed in duplicate and delivered to the Trustee. If there is more than one beneficiary, the remaining beneficiaries must first approve of said transfer in writing. The remaining beneficiaries shall have a sixty (60) day right of first refusal to purchase said interest. Unless stated otherwise, any assignment of beneficial interest hereunder shall also include the power of direction and revocation of this trust agreement. Any beneficiary who assigns his interest in full shall forever waive his right to revoke this trust agreement.

18. <u>Individual Liability of Trustee</u>. The Trustee shall not be required, in dealing with the Trust Property or in otherwise acting under this

Agreement, to enter into any individual contract or other individual obligation whatsoever; nor to make itself individually liable to pay or incur the payment of any damages, attorneys' fees, fines, penalties, forfeitures, costs, charges or other sums of money whatsoever. The Trustee shall have no individual liability or obligation whatsoever arising from its ownership, as Trustee, of the legal title to the Trust Property, or with respect to any act done or contract entered into or indebtedness incurred by it in dealing with the Trust Property or in otherwise acting under this Agreement, except only as far as the Trust Property and any trust funds in the actual possession of the Trustee shall be applicable to the payment and discharge of that liability or obligation.

19. Reimbursement and Indemnification of Trustee. If the Trustee shall pay or incur any liability to pay any money on account of this Trust, or incur any liability to pay any money on account of being made a party to any litigation as a result of holding title to the Trust Property or otherwise in connection with this Trust the Beneficiaries, jointly and severally, agree that on demand they will pay to the Trustee all such payments made or liabilities incurred by the Trustee, together with its expenses, including reasonable attorneys' fees, and that they will indemnify and hold the Trustee harmless of and from any and all payments made or liabilities incurred by it for any reason whatsoever as a result of this Agreement.

20. Unanimous Direction of Beneficiaries. Wherever an act, decision or direction is required by the "Beneficiary" or "Beneficiaries" herein, said designation shall be deemed to mean all of the beneficiaries acting in a unanimous agreement, unless a lesser percentage is so specified.

21. Governing Law. This agreement, and all transactions contemplated hereby, shall be governed by, construed and enforced in accordance with the laws of the State of _____. The parties herein waive trial by jury and agree to submit to the personal jurisdiction and venue of a court of subject matter jurisdiction located in the County in which the property sits. In the event that litigation results from or arises out of this Agreement or the performance thereof, the parties agree to reimburse the prevailing party's reasonable attorney's fees, court costs, and all other expenses, whether or not taxable by the court as costs, in addition to any other relief to which the prevailing party may be entitled. In such event, no action shall be entertained by said court or any court of competent jurisdiction if filed more than one year subsequent to the date the cause(s) of action actually accrued regardless of whether damages were otherwise as of said time calculable.

22. <u>Binding Effect</u>. The terms and conditions of this Agreement shall inure to the benefit of and be binding upon any successor trustee under it, as well as upon the executors, administrators, heirs, assigns and all other successors in interest of the Beneficiaries.

23. <u>Annual Statements</u>. There shall be no annual meeting of the Beneficiaries, but the Trustee shall prepare an annual report of their receipts and disbursements for the fiscal year preceding, which fiscal year shall coincide with the calendar year, and a copy of the report shall be sent by mail to the Beneficiaries not later than February 28 of each year.

24. <u>Termination of this Agreement</u>. This Trust may be terminated on thirty (30) days written notice signed by all of beneficiaries and delivered to the Trustee. Upon the termination of this Agreement, the Trustee shall deliver all books, records, bank account information, keys, security deposits, leases and funds in his or her possession, and execute any documents necessary to convey title to the trust property to the beneficiaries as their interests may appear.

25. <u>Entire Agreement</u>. This Agreement contains the entire understanding between the parties and may be amended, revoked or terminated only by written agreement signed by the Trustee and all of the Beneficiaries.

IN WITNESS WHEREOF, the parties hereto have executed this agreement as of the day and year first above written.

The beneficiaries:

_____

_____

_____

_____

STATE OF_____)

)ss:

COUNTY OF _____)

On _____, 20____ , before me, _____, a
notary public in and for said state personally appeared
, personally known to me (or proved to me based upon satisfactory
evidence) to be the person(s) whose name(s) are subscribed to the within
instrument and acknowledged that (s)he/they executed the same in
his/her/their signature on the instrument the person(s) or entity on behalf of
which they acted, executed the instrument.

Witness my hand and official seal

_____

NOTARY PUBLIC

My commission expires _____

[NOTARY
SEAL]

The Trustees:

_____

_____

STATE OF_____)

)ss:

COUNTY OF _____)

On _____, 20_____ , before me, _____, a notary public in and for said state personally appeared
, personally known to me (or proved to me based upon satisfactory evidence) to be the person(s) whose name(s) are subscribed to the within instrument and acknowledged that (s)he/they executed the same in his/her/their signature on the instrument the person(s) or entity on behalf of which they acted, executed the instrument.

Witness my hand and official seal

_____

NOTARY PUBLIC

My commission expires _____

[NOTARY SEAL]

EXHIBIT "A"

TRUST PROPERTY

Known by street and address as:

EXHIBIT "B"

BENEFICIARIES AND THEIR INTERESTS

Name and Address   %
Interest

ASSIGNMENT OF THE BENEFICIAL INTEREST

ASSIGNMENT OF THE BENEFICIAL INTEREST

DATE: _____

FOR VALUE RECEIVED, the undersigned assignor(s) hereby sell(s), assign(n), transfer(s) and set(s) over unto _____ assignee(s), _____ percent (_____%) of the assignor's rights, power, privileges and beneficial interest in and to that certain trust agreement dated _____and known as _____ including all interest in the property held subject to said trust agreement.

The real property constituting the corpus of the land trust:

Address _____

The power of direction shall be held by

_____

Signature of Assignor(s)

_____

Signature

_____

Printed Name

SSN/EIN _____

ACCEPTANCE BY ASSIGNEE
The undersigned assignee(s) accept the foregoing assignment subject to all the provisions of said trust agreement.
Signature(s) of Assignee(s)

_____

Signature

Printed Name _____

SSN/EIN _____

_____Address
City, State, Zip

Phone _____

CONSENT OF COLLATERAL ASSIGNEE (if APPLICABLE)

_____
Name of Lender (please note successor information if applicable)

By: _____

Its: _____
    Title

RECEIPT BY TRUSTEE

Received and acknowledged the foregoing assignment and acceptance.

Date: _____

By Trustee: _____

Signature:

_____
Trustee

OPTION AGREEMENT FOR PURCHASE OF REAL PROPERTY

OPTION AGREEMENT FOR PURCHASE OF REAL PROPERTY

THIS OPTION AGREEMENT ("Agreement") made and entered into this _____ day of _____, 200_,

By and between _____,

Whose principal address is

_____, hereinafter

referred to as "Seller"

And _____,

whose principal address is

_____, hereinafter referred to

as "Purchaser":

W I T N E S S:

WHEREAS, Seller is the fee simple owner of certain real property being, lying and situated in the County of _____, State of _____, such real property having the street address of:

_____

WHEREAS, Purchaser desires to procure an option to purchase the Premises upon the terms and provisions as hereinafter set forth;

NOW, THEREFORE, for good and valuable consideration the receipt and sufficiency of which is hereby acknowledged by the parties hereto and for the mutual covenants contained herein, Seller and Purchaser hereby agree as follows:

1. DEFINITIONS. For the purposes of this Agreement, the following terms shall have the following meanings:

(a) "Execution Date" shall mean the day upon which the last party to this Agreement shall duly execute this Agreement;

(b) "Option Fee" shall mean the total sum of a down payment of
_____ plus all closing costs, payable as set forth below;

(c) "Option Term" shall mean that period of time commencing on the
Execution Date and ending on or before _____, 20____;

(d) "Option Exercise Date" shall mean that date, within the Option Term,
upon which the Purchaser shall send its written notice to Seller exercising
its Option to Purchase;

(e) "Closing Date" shall mean the last day of the closing term or such other
date during the closing term selected by Purchaser.

2. GRANT OF OPTION. For and in consideration of the Option Fee
payable to Seller as set forth herein, Seller does hereby grant to Purchaser
the exclusive right and Option ("Option") to purchase the premises upon the
terms and conditions as set forth herein.

3. PAYMENT OF OPTION FEE. Purchaser agrees to pay the Seller a
down payment of _____ plus all closing costs upon the
Execution Date.

4. EXERCISE OF OPTION. Purchaser may exercise its exclusive right to
purchase the Premises pursuant to the Option, at any time during the Option
Term, by giving written notice thereof to Seller. As provided for above, the
date of sending of said notice shall be the Option Exercise Date. In the
event the Purchaser does not exercise its exclusive right to purchase the
Premises granted by the Option during the Option Term, Seller shall be
entitled to retain the Option Fee, and this agreement shall become
absolutely null and void and neither party hereto shall have any other
liability, obligation or duty herein under or pursuant to this Agreement.

5. CONTRACT FOR PURCHASE & SALE OF REAL PROPERTY. In the event that the Purchaser exercises its exclusive Option as provided for in the preceding paragraph, Seller agrees to sell and Purchaser agrees to buy the Premises and both parties agree to execute a contract for such purchase and sale of the Premises in accordance with the following terms and conditions:

(a) Purchase Price. The total purchase price for the Premises shall be the sum of _____ ($_____); however, Purchaser shall receive a credit toward such purchase price in the amount of the Option Fee thus, purchase price shall at that time be adjusted accordingly.

(b) Closing Date. The closing date shall be on _____, 20____ or at any other date during the Option Term as may be selected by Purchaser;

(c) Closing Costs. Purchaser's and Seller's costs of closing the Contract shall be borne by Purchaser and shall be prepaid as a portion of the Option Fee;

(d) Default by Purchaser; Remedies of Seller. In the event Purchaser, after exercise of the Option, fails to proceed with the closing of the purchase of the Premises pursuant to the terms and provisions as contained herein and/or under the Contract, Seller shall be entitled to retain the Option Fee as liquidated damages and shall have no further recourse against Purchaser;

(e) Default by Seller; Remedies of Purchaser. In the event Seller fails to close the sale of the Premises pursuant to the terms and provisions of this Agreement and/or under the Contract, Purchaser shall be entitled to either sue for specific performance of the real estate purchase and sale contract or terminate such Contract and sue for money damages.

6. MISCELLANEOUS.

(a) Execution by Both Parties. This Agreement shall not become effective and binding until fully executed by both Purchaser and Seller.

(b) Notice. All notices, demands and/or consents provided for in this Agreement shall be in writing and shall be delivered to the parties hereto by hand or by United States Mail with postage pre-paid. Such notices shall be deemed to have been served on the date mailed, postage pre-paid. All such notices and communications shall be addressed to the Seller at
_____ and to Purchaser at
_____or at such other address as either may specify to the other in writing.

(c) Fee Governing Law. This Agreement shall be governed by and construed in accordance with the laws of the State of Tennessee.

(d) Successors and Assigns. This Agreement shall apply to, inure to the benefit of and be binding upon and enforceable against the parties hereto and their respective heirs, successors, and/or assigns, to the extent as if specified at length throughout this Agreement.

(e) Time. Time is of the essence of this Agreement.

(f) Headings. The headings inserted at the beginning of each paragraph and/or subparagraph are for convenience of reference only and shall not limit or otherwise affect or be used in the construction of any terms or provisions hereof.

(g) Cost of this Agreement. Any cost and/or fees incurred by the Purchaser or Seller in executing this Agreement shall be borne by the respective party incurring such cost and/or fee.

(h) Entire Agreement. This Agreement contains all of the terms, promises, covenants, conditions and representations made or entered into by or between Seller and Purchaser and supersedes all prior discussions and agreements whether written or oral between Seller and Purchaser with respect to the Option and all other matters contained herein and constitutes the sole and entire agreement between Seller and Purchaser with respect thereto. This Agreement may not be modified or amended unless such amendment is set forth in writing and executed by both Seller and Purchaser with the formalities hereof.

IN WITNESS WHEREOF, the parties hereto have caused this Agreement to be executed under proper authority:

As to Purchaser this _____ day of _____, 20_____.

Witnesses: "Purchaser"

_____

_____

As to Seller this _____ day of _____, 20____.

Witnesses: "Seller"

_____

_____

ESTATE LETTER

Date:

Name

Address

Dear   ,

I would like to offer my condolences on the recent loss of your loved one, as I am aware that this is a difficult time for both you and your family.

My name is   and I am the principle probate real estate investor with   LLC. I provide valuable services that may be of benefit to you.

I buy real estate both residential and commercial, paying all CASH with quick closing. I purchase properties in their "as is" condition, which helps you avoid costly repairs to qualify the property for financing.

I purchase real estate contracts, notes, mortgages and other types of accounts receivables, automobiles, jewelry, or anything of value.

I can also help get the property cleaned out, cleaned and prepared to get it ready to sell.

When working with me, you will be dealing with a principle who has the cash immediately available. I can enable you to settle the estate more quickly by saving you time in selling the probate property, this resulting in much lower legal costs and holding expenses.

Because of the possible sensitive timing for settling the estate, just call and let me know what you want price-wise, I will be more than happy to make you an offer.

Of course you are under no obligation. You really have nothing to lose by at least seeing what I am willing to pay. Please feel free to call me at   if you have any questions and would like to discuss selling the property, the contents or both.

Sincerely,

PS. Please keep in mind that you do not have to wait the eight month probate period before you call me to discuss.

Don't forget to go access MY WHOLESALING VAULT at <u>mywholesalingvault.com</u>

<u>The following pages left blank for</u>

<u>notes</u>

Made in the USA
Monee, IL
14 June 2023

35788256R00115